BANKING THE BUSINESS

Where Retail Banking Ends and Business Banking Begins

Chad W. Maze

First edition

Published by **Discipline of Banking Press**
United States of America

ISBN: 979-8-9956359-3-2 (paperback)
ISBN: 979-8-9956359-4-9 (eBook)
ISBN: 979-8-9956359-5-6 (audiobook)
Library of Congress Control Number: 2026909313

LEGAL DISCLAIMER This book is provided for informational and educational purposes only. It does not constitute legal, regulatory, accounting, tax, investment, or financial advice. The author and publisher make no representations or warranties regarding the accuracy, completeness, or applicability of the content to any specific institution, transaction, or circumstance. Readers should consult qualified professional advisors before making decisions that may affect their institution, organization, or personal financial situation. The views expressed in this book are those of the author and do not necessarily reflect the views of any employer, board, institution, regulator, or organization with which the author is or has been affiliated. References to laws, regulations, supervisory guidance, or industry practices are provided for general context only and may change over time.

Printed in the United States of America

Discipline of Banking Press is an imprint of Camino De Oro Enterprises, LLC.

ACKNOWLEDGEMENTS

A quick note on terms before we start. In this book I use "commercial banking" and "business banking" interchangeably. The industry usually draws a line between small business banking and commercial lending, different teams, different thresholds, different rooms. That line matters in some places. It doesn't here. Whatever you call it, business banking, commercial banking, middle market, C&I, it's a different animal than banking consumers. That's the work these pages are about.

Commercial banking is a discipline built in rooms most people never see, credit committees, loan reviews, difficult conversations with borrowers, navigating hard moments. The understanding in these pages came from those rooms, and from the people in them.

I am grateful to the business owners who trusted me with their financials, their plans, and occasionally their fears. The deals that worked taught me what sound structure looks like. The ones that didn't taught me what I should have asked earlier. Both kinds are in this book.

I am grateful to the credit professionals who pushed back on deals I brought them and were right to do so. There is no better education in commercial lending than having someone with more experience ask the question you didn't think to ask.

And I am grateful to the bankers I have hired, developed, and watched grow into this discipline over thirty years. This book exists because of the questions they asked, the ones that showed me which parts of this work are genuinely difficult to teach, and which parts simply haven't been taught well enough.

Banking the Business is the attempt to do it better.

Chad W. Maze

TABLE OF CONTENTS

PROLOGUE

Before We Begin

There is a banker somewhere right now sitting across from a business owner.

Maybe it's a first meeting. Maybe the business owner was referred by someone who said this banker was worth talking to. Maybe the conversation started about a checking account and drifted, naturally, toward something bigger, a building they've been thinking about buying, an equipment need they've been putting off, a growth opportunity that keeps presenting itself and keeps getting deferred because the capital isn't there.

The business owner is telling a story. Their story. The story of how the business started, what it has become, where they want it to go, and what they need from a banking partner to get there.

And the banker, depending on where they are in their development, is either hearing that story or waiting for the part where they can match it to a product.

This book is for the banker who wants to hear the story.

* * *

Not because hearing stories is a soft skill that makes banking feel warmer. But because in commercial banking, the story is the job. It is the first discipline, the organizing principle, and the ultimate test of whether a banker understands the credit they are about to evaluate. A banker who can tell the story of a deal, clearly, completely, and confidently, before a single financial statement has been reviewed has already done something that no spreadsheet can replicate. They have made a judgment. They have decided whether the relationship makes sense before they have asked the numbers to carry that weight.

That judgment is what this book is about.

* * *

Banking the Business was written for a specific banker at a specific moment in their career. They are good at what they do. They have spent real time in banking, learning the products, building relationships, developing instincts about people and money and the rhythms of financial life. They are not starting from scratch. They start from a foundation that is real and valuable and genuinely worth building on.

But they are making a transition. From retail to commercial. From consumer to business. From a world where the product is standardized and the decision is largely algorithmic to a world where nothing is pulled off a shelf and everything is built around the specific needs and specific risks of a specific business at a specific point in its life.

That transition is not small. And it is not just technical.

The technical skills, reading a financial statement, calculating a DSCR, evaluating collateral, are learnable. They are introduced in this book and developed fully in the books that follow. But the technical skills sit on top of something that has to come first: a fundamental reorientation of how a banker approaches the work. From transaction to relationship. From product to custom-built solution. From approval as the goal to the right decision as the standard.

That reorientation is what the retail-to-commercial transition actually requires. And it is what this book is designed to support.

* * *

A few things worth knowing before you begin.

This book does not assume you know nothing. It assumes you know something, and that what you know is a foundation worth building on, not a liability worth apologizing for. Every chapter in this book starts from where a good retail banker already stands and moves forward from there. The instincts that made you effective in retail banking will not disappear when you move into commercial banking.

They will be redirected, refined, and put to work in a more complex environment, one that rewards exactly the kind of genuine curiosity, relationship discipline, and honest communication that good retail banking builds.

This book does not try to teach you everything. It tries to teach you the right things first, the foundation that every other piece of commercial banking knowledge sits on. The financial statement literacy, the credit framework, the structural logic, and the practitioner mindset that together constitute the entry point to the discipline. When you finish this book, you will not be a fully formed commercial banker. You will be a banker who is ready to become one, which is a different and more useful thing.

This book does not pretend that commercial banking is more complicated than it needs to be. It is complex, genuinely, substantively complex, in ways that reward years of study and practice. But complexity is not the same as obscurity. The concepts that drive commercial credit analysis are not mysterious. They are logical. They build on each other. They make sense when they are explained clearly and in the right order. That is what this book attempts to do, explain the right things in the right order, in plain language, without unnecessary jargon, and without the false comfort of oversimplification.

* * *

There is a moment that experienced commercial bankers describe, and it comes for everyone who stays in the discipline long enough. It is the moment when a borrower walks in and before the file is opened, before the financial statements are reviewed, before the formal analysis begins, the banker already has a sense of the deal. Not a conclusion. A sense. A preliminary orientation formed from the story the borrower told, the way they told it, the consistency between the narrative and what the banker knows about the industry, and the accumulated pattern recognition of a career spent evaluating businesses and the people who run them.

That sense is not magic. It is not instinct in the mystical sense. It is the product of everything in this book, applied repeatedly, reflected on honestly, and refined across years of practice until it becomes second nature.

You are at the beginning of building that sense.

This book is where it starts.

* * *

One more thing.

The business owner sitting across from that banker right now, the one telling their story, is hoping for something specific. Not just capital. Not just a competitive rate. Not just a bank that processes their application without losing their documents.

They are hoping for a banker who actually understands their business. Who listens to the story before reaching for the product. Who asks the right questions, builds something custom, and shows up not just at closing but across the full arc of the relationship.

That banker exists. They are in every institution that takes commercial banking seriously. And with the right foundation, the right understanding of how this discipline works and what it asks of the people who practice it, that banker could be you.

Go learn the story.

Everything else follows from there.

INTRODUCTION

You're Already in the Room, Now Learn to Read It

There's a moment that happens to almost every retail banker who makes the move into commercial lending. It happens in a meeting, or during a loan review, or sometimes just sitting alone with a financial statement they've been handed like it should mean something obvious.

The moment is this: *I don't know what I'm looking at.*

Not because they aren't smart. Not because they haven't worked hard. But because everything they learned about lending, the approvals, the declines, the credit scores, the debt-to-income ratios, the checklists, was built for a completely different kind of borrower. A consumer. An individual. Someone whose financial life fits inside a pay stub and a credit report.

The business borrower doesn't fit there. And the loan that funds that business doesn't work the way a mortgage or an auto loan works. The rules are different. The questions are different. The risks are different. And the way a lender has to*think*, that's different too.

This book exists because that gap is real, it's common, and it's rarely addressed directly.

It Usually Starts Before the Loan

Here's something worth understanding before you read another word about credit: most business banking relationships don't begin with a loan.

They begin with a conversation. A business owner walks into a branch, or calls, or gets referred, and what they need first is a place to put their money. A business checking account. Maybe a way to accept payments. Payroll. Online banking for their bookkeeper. Cash management tools that help them see where their money is going.

That's the entry point. And if you've spent time in a branch, there's a good chance you've already had that conversation. You opened the account. You set up the services. You became, without necessarily knowing it, the beginning of a business banking relationship.

What many retail bankers don't realize in that moment is that the deposit relationship and the lending relationship are not two separate things. They are two expressions of the same thing, a financial partnership with a business. The deposits reflect how the business operates day to day. The loans reflect where the business is trying to go. Together, they tell the story of what the business is, how it's managed, and whether it's the kind of relationship worth deepening.

This is the foundation of commercial banking. Not the credit memo. Not the collateral. Not the debt service coverage ratio. The relationship, built first on trust, usually opened with a deposit account, and eventually extended into credit when the time is right and the risk makes sense.

Understanding this changes how you approach the work. A retail banker who sees a business checking account as a transaction will miss the signals sitting right in front of them. A banker who sees it as the first chapter of a longer story will ask better questions, notice more, and be far better positioned when the conversation eventually turns to lending.

That shift in perspective, from transaction to relationship, from product to partnership, is where this book begins.

Tell the Story First

Before the numbers. Before the documents. Before the credit memo, the collateral valuation, or the debt service calculation, tell the story.

This is the first discipline of commercial banking, and it is the one most often skipped.

Every deal has a story. Who is this borrower? What do they do, and how do they actually make money? Why are they here, and what are they asking for? Why does this request make sense, for them, and for your institution? And why does this relationship belong on your books?

If you can answer those questions in plain language before you open a spreadsheet or pull a credit report, you understand the deal. If you can't, you're not ready to present it, and more importantly, you're not ready to defend it.

The story test is not just a communication tool. It's a thinking tool. A banker who leads with the story has done something the numbers alone can never do: they've made a judgment. They've decided whether the relationship makes sense before they've asked the credit to carry that weight. And they've signaled to every senior lender or credit officer in the room that they understand what they're bringing forward.

Throughout this book, you'll be asked to think in stories before you think in spreadsheets. That's not a soft idea. It's the discipline that separates bankers who process deals from bankers who understand them. In commercial banking, the story comes first. Everything else follows.

What This Book Is

Banking the Business is a commercial lending primer. It is not a textbook. It is not a compliance manual. It is not a collection of formulas to memorize or regulations to recite. It is a practitioner's introduction to how commercial bankers think, written for people who already understand banking but haven't yet learned to see a loan, a deposit relationship, or a business borrower the way an experienced commercial banker sees them.

If you are a retail branch banker exploring a move into business banking, this book was written for you. If you are a new commercial lender in your first two years and you feel like everyone around you speaks a language you're still translating, this book was written for you. If you work at a credit union and your institution is building out its commercial lending capacity and you need to understand the fundamentals before you can contribute meaningfully, this book was written for you. And if you're a universal banker or a relationship manager expected to hold both consumer and commercial conversations with the same confidence, this book was written for you too.

The common thread isn't your title. It's your situation: you're already in the room. You just need to learn to read it.

What You'll Learn

This book is organized in three parts.

Part One is about the shift. Before you can understand commercial lending mechanics, you have to understand why commercial lending is fundamentally different from what you've been trained to do. The business borrower is not a consumer. A business loan is not a bigger personal loan. And the instincts that make a great retail banker can actually work against you in commercial credit if you don't understand where they apply and where they don't.

Part Two is about the numbers. Not accounting, you don't need a degree in finance to read this section. But you do need to understand what the income statement is telling you, what the balance sheet reveals about risk, and why the most dangerous sentence in commercial lending is *"the business is profitable."* Profit and cash flow are not the same thing. That distinction alone has saved careers, and when missed, ended them.

Part Three is about how a deal comes together. From the first conversation with a borrower to the structure of the loan itself to the mindset a lender carries into every credit decision, this section walks you through the lending lifecycle at the level you need before you can go deeper.

Along the way, you'll be introduced to a framework I call the*5 Cs and a G*, the six lenses every commercial lender uses to evaluate a credit request. You've probably heard of the 5 Cs. The G is the one most training programs skip. It won't be skipped here.

What This Book Is Not

This is a starting point, not a destination.

Banking the Business will give you the foundation, the vocabulary, the mental models, and the practitioner instincts you need to begin thinking like a commercial banker. What it will not give you is the full framework. The deep credit mechanics, the loan type disciplines, and the deal architecture that define a great commercial lender live in *Loan by Design*™. The deposit strategy, cash management philosophy, and the discipline of building and retaining business deposits live in *The Cash Discipline.*

This book is the prerequisite to both. Think of it as the common ground, the place where the lending path and the deposit path share the same foundation before they diverge into their own disciplines.

By the time you finish the last chapter here, you'll be ready to choose your next step, or take both.

A Word on How to Read This

Each chapter in this book is short by design. Commercial lending rewards precision, and so does good instruction. You won't find padding here. What you will find, in every chapter, are the concepts that actually matter, explained the way a senior lender would explain them to someone they're genuinely trying to develop, not someone they're trying to impress.

Read it straight through the first time. Then go back to the chapters that challenge you most. By the end, you should feel something specific: not mastery, that comes later, but readiness. The readiness to ask better questions, read a financial statement without panic, walk into a borrower conversation with a lender's eye, and tell the story of a deal before you ever open the file.

That's the goal. Let's get to work.

PART ONE

How Commercial Lending Is Different

Before you can understand commercial lending mechanics, you have to understand why commercial lending is fundamentally different from what you've been trained to do. The business borrower is not a consumer. A business loan is not a bigger personal loan. And the instincts that make a great retail banker can actually work against you in commercial credit, if you don't understand where they apply and where they don't.

Part One draws that line clearly. It explains what you bring into commercial banking that is genuinely valuable, what you need to leave behind, and why the shift from a transaction mindset to a credit mindset is not just a vocabulary change, it is a complete reorientation of how you approach the work.

Three chapters. One foundational shift. Everything else builds from here.

CHAPTER 1

You Already Know More Than You Think

Let's start with something that doesn't get said often enough in commercial banking training programs: you already know more than you think.

Not everything. Not even most of it. But more than you're being given credit for, and more than you're probably giving yourself credit for.

If you've spent time in a branch, you've had thousands of conversations about money. You've helped people open accounts, navigate overdrafts, apply for loans, plan for large purchases, and manage the financial machinery of their daily lives. You've learned how to read a person in the first five minutes of a conversation. You've developed instincts about who follows through and who doesn't. You've sat across from people in difficult financial situations and found a way to be both honest and constructive. You've learned the language of compliance without becoming paralyzed by it. And you've done all of this while managing a line of customers, hitting product goals, and keeping your drawer balanced.

That is not nothing. That is a foundation.

The problem isn't that retail banking teaches you the wrong things. The problem is that it teaches you a specific set of things, and then commercial banking asks you to do something those things weren't designed for. The skills transfer, but the application changes. And if nobody explains where the boundaries are, you'll spend the first year of your commercial banking career trying to apply retail logic to commercial problems and wondering why it keeps not quite working.

This chapter is about drawing that line clearly, so you know what to bring with you and what to leave at the door.

What You Bring With You

The move into commercial banking is not a reinvention. It's a reapplication. Many of the skills that made you effective in retail banking are directly relevant in commercial banking, they just need to be redirected.

Relationship instincts. In retail banking, you learned to build trust quickly. You learned that people do business with people they feel comfortable with, and that the quality of a conversation often matters as much as the quality of the product. That instinct doesn't change in commercial banking, it amplifies. Business owners are frequently approached by multiple banks. They are often skeptical of bankers who lead with pitches and feel-good promises. What earns their trust is the same thing that earned your retail customers' trust: genuine interest, honest communication, and the sense that you understand their situation before you start offering solutions. Your retail instincts got you in the room. They'll keep you there.

Compliance awareness. Commercial banking operates inside the same regulatory environment you already understand, Bank Secrecy Act, Know Your Customer requirements, fair lending obligations. You won't need to start from scratch. What you'll find is that the compliance landscape in commercial banking has its own layer of complexity, particularly around entity documentation, beneficial ownership, and loan covenants. But the underlying discipline, follow the rules, document everything, ask when you're unsure, is exactly the same. You already have that discipline. That matters more than you might think.

Financial familiarity with an important correction. You understand how financial instruments work at a mechanical level. You know what a line of credit is. You understand amortization, collateral, and the concept of a personal guarantee. That foundation is real and useful. But here is where the framing has to change: in retail banking, these things are called *products*, standardized offerings designed to fit a broad category of customer need. In business banking and commercial lending, nothing is pulled off a shelf. Everything is custom built. The line of credit a contractor needs to bridge payroll between draws is not the same instrument as the line of credit a medical practice needs to manage billing cycle gaps, even if they look similar on a term sheet. The mechanics transfer. The mindset of matching a product to a customer does not. In commercial banking, you build around the business. You don't fit the business into the product.

Reading people. This is underrated in formal training but invaluable in practice. Commercial banking involves a significant amount of judgment about character, not just financial character, but personal character. Is this borrower straightforward? Do they own their problems or deflect them? Do they understand their own business, or are they guessing? Do they have the management capacity to execute what they're proposing? These are not questions you answer with a spreadsheet. They're questions you answer by paying close attention during a conversation, something you've been doing for years.

The ability to have a hard conversation. Retail banking trains you to deliver unwelcome news. A declined loan application. An account that has to be closed. A service that isn't available. You've learned to have those conversations with professionalism and empathy. That skill is directly applicable in commercial banking, where the stakes are higher and the conversations are sometimes harder. A banker who has never learned to say no clearly and without apology is not equipped for commercial credit.

What Doesn't Transfer

Here is where it gets important. The instincts and habits that follow will serve you well in a consumer banking context. In commercial banking, they can lead you in exactly the wrong direction if you don't recognize them for what they are.

The credit score reflex. In consumer lending, the credit score is a primary decision-making tool. It's fast, it's standardized, and for a personal loan or a credit card, it tells you most of what you need to know about a borrower's repayment behavior. When you move into commercial lending, the credit score becomes one data point among many, and often not the most important one. A business with a strong credit score can still fail to generate enough cash flow to service its debt. Reaching for the credit score first is a retail habit. Commercial lenders reach for the cash flow first.

The debt-to-income instinct. Consumer underwriting is largely built around the debt-to-income ratio. In commercial lending, the equivalent question is more nuanced, not just how much the business earns, but how it earns it, how consistently it earns it, what happens to those earnings when conditions change, and whether the loan being requested will be repaid from the business's operating cash flow or from some other source. The DTI reflex is too blunt an instrument for that kind of analysis.

The checklist mentality. Retail lending is largely a checklist-driven process. Commercial lending requires that same discipline around documentation and process, but it also requires something the checklist can't provide: judgment. Two businesses can have identical financial ratios and represent completely different levels of risk depending on industry, management experience, competitive position, and market conditions. A commercial banker who processes deals through a checklist without exercising judgment is not doing the job. They're doing half of it.

Approval as the goal. In retail banking, the path to a successful customer interaction often ends with an approval. In commercial banking, the goal is not the approval, it's the right decision. Sometimes the right decision is a decline. Sometimes it's an approval with conditions the borrower didn't expect. A commercial banker who is oriented toward approval as the goal will eventually approve something they shouldn't, because the approval felt like success rather than the outcome being the success.

Retail Products Are Standardized. Commercial Lending Is Custom Built.

At some point early in the transition from retail to commercial banking, the language changes, and the language change matters.

In retail banking, the word is *products*. Products are designed to be standardized. They are built once, offered broadly, and selected by the customer based on their individual need. The banker's job is to match the right product to the right customer and execute the transaction cleanly. That is a legitimate and valuable skill. But it is a fundamentally different orientation than what commercial banking requires.

In business banking and commercial lending, nothing is pulled off a shelf. A commercial credit facility, a cash management structure, a deposit and lending relationship designed around how a business actually operates, these are custom built. The business tells you how it works, what it needs, where it's going, and what gaps it needs a banking partner to fill. Your job is to listen carefully enough to build something that actually fits, and to understand the credit well enough to know whether your institution should be the one building it.

Here is what makes that question so powerful in commercial banking: the answer is almost always yes, if the risk can be quantified and the structure works for both the borrower and the institution.

That is not a small thing. In retail banking, the product limits the possible. The structure is fixed. In commercial banking, the structure is not fixed, it is designed. If a banker can understand the business well enough to identify what it actually needs, analyze the risk well enough to quantify it honestly, and build a structure that serves the borrower's purpose while protecting the institution's position, that structure can be built. The freedom to design rather than select is one of the defining features of commercial banking. And it comes with a corresponding responsibility: the discipline to build only what the risk actually supports.

Custom built is not a license to approve anything a borrower asks for. It is the responsibility to understand the need completely, quantify the risk honestly, and build something that genuinely works, for the borrower and for the institution. Both conditions matter. A structure that serves the borrower but exposes the institution to unquantified risk is not a good commercial loan. A structure that protects the institution but doesn't actually meet the borrower's need is not a good commercial relationship. The standard is mutual benefit.

The shift from product to custom built is not just a vocabulary change. It is a complete reorientation of how you approach the work, from fitting customers into structures to building structures around customers. It is one of the first things an experienced commercial banker will notice about how you think. And it is one of the clearest signals that you're ready for this work.

The Shift: From Transaction to Credit Mindset

At the center of everything in this chapter is a single shift, and it's less about skills than about orientation.

In retail banking, you were trained to match a product to a need. Someone needs a car loan; you help them get a car loan. The transaction is the unit of work. Your job is to execute it well.

In commercial banking, the unit of work is the relationship, and the credit decision is not a transaction. It's a judgment about whether your institution should enter a financial partnership with a business, extend capital to that business, and trust that the business will generate enough cash flow to repay it.

This is the credit mindset. It doesn't arrive all at once. It develops over time, with exposure to deals, mistakes, mentors, and the accumulated experience of sitting across from enough borrowers to start recognizing patterns. But it starts with understanding that commercial banking asks a different question than retail banking.

Retail banking asks: *does this person qualify?*

Commercial banking asks: *does this make sense?*

That is not a small distinction. It is the entire job.

The Story Is Already There

Every business that walks through your door, or calls, or gets referred, has a story. How it started. What it does. How it makes money. Where it's trying to go. What it needs from a banking relationship to get there. That story existed before the loan request, and it will continue long after the loan is made or declined.

Your job as a commercial banker is to understand that story, not just to process the transaction that's in front of you today. And the remarkable thing about that job is that you've actually been practicing for it since the first day you sat down across from a customer and asked how you could help.

You were listening to stories then. You just weren't calling them that.

You already know more than you think. The chapters ahead will show you how to use it.

> *Practitioner's Note: The most common mistake retail bankers make in their first year of commercial banking is not a technical mistake. It's an orientation mistake, continuing to think in products and transactions when the job requires thinking in custom-built relationships and credit judgments. The technical skills are learnable. The mindset shift is the work.*

CHAPTER 2

The Business Borrower Is Not a Consumer

If you take one thing from this chapter, take this: the business borrower is not a larger, more complicated version of a consumer borrower. They are a fundamentally different kind of borrower, with different motivations, different risks, different financial structures, and a completely different relationship to the money they're asking you to lend.

This distinction sounds obvious when it's stated plainly. But it is violated constantly, by new commercial bankers who default to consumer logic because it's what they know, by institutions that try to standardize commercial underwriting the way they standardize consumer underwriting, and by training programs that teach the 5 Cs without explaining why those questions exist in the first place.

The reason those questions exist is because the business borrower is different. Understanding how and why they're different is the foundation of everything else in this book.

The Borrower Isn't Always Who You Think

In consumer lending, the borrower is a person. There may be a co-borrower, but the credit relationship is fundamentally between your institution and an individual human being with a Social Security number, a credit history, a job, and a monthly income. The identity of the borrower is rarely ambiguous.

In commercial lending, the borrower is often an entity, and the entity is not the same thing as the person who walks into your office.

Business entities come in several common forms, and each one carries a different legal and financial structure that affects how credit risk is evaluated.

A sole proprietorship is the simplest structure. There is no legal separation between the business and the owner. The owner and the business are, for most practical purposes, the same. Credit risk and personal risk are inseparable. This is the structure where consumer and commercial credit blur most closely together.

A partnership involves two or more individuals sharing ownership of a business. General partnerships carry unlimited personal liability for all partners. Limited partnerships designate at least one general partner with full liability and one or more limited partners whose exposure is capped at their investment.

A limited liability company, or LLC, is the most common structure you will encounter in commercial banking. The LLC creates a legal separation between the business and its owners, called members. That separation limits the personal liability of the members. But it also means you are evaluating a credit relationship with a legal entity, not a person.

A corporation, whether a standard C-corp or an S-corp, is the most formally structured business entity. Corporations have shareholders, boards, officers, bylaws, and a legal identity entirely separate from the people who own and operate them. S-corporations pass income and losses through to shareholders' personal tax returns, which means you'll often find business income reported on a personal tax return rather than a standalone business return.

Why does all of this matter? Because the entity structure tells you something important before you've looked at a single financial statement. It tells you how the business is organized, who is responsible for its obligations, and what legal protections exist between the business and its owners.

In commercial lending, the legal separation between a business entity and its owners is real, but it is frequently bridged by a personal commitment from the owner, someone who agrees to be personally responsible if the business cannot perform. That person, and what they bring to the credit picture, is one of the most important dimensions of commercial credit analysis. We will return to it in Chapter 3, where the full framework for evaluating a commercial credit request is introduced.

How Business Borrowers Think

A consumer borrower comes to a bank with a specific need and a request sized to that need. The request is personal. The repayment comes from their income. The relationship is largely transactional.

A business borrower operates on an entirely different set of motivations.

Business owners borrow to grow. They borrow to bridge gaps between when they deliver and when they get paid. They borrow to buy equipment that generates more revenue than it costs to finance. They borrow to acquire other businesses, fund construction, manage seasonal swings in cash flow, or take advantage of opportunities that require capital before the revenue to justify it has fully materialized.

The relationship between a business borrower and their bank is not transactional, or it shouldn't be. It is ongoing, evolving, and layered. Today it may be a line of credit to manage cash flow. In two years it may be a term loan to buy a building. In five years it may be an acquisition facility to purchase a competitor.

This is why the business banking relationship begins before the loan request, often long before. The deposit account, the cash management structure, the merchant services relationship, these are not separate from the credit relationship. They are the foundation of it. A banker who understands this will invest in a business relationship before there is anything to underwrite. A banker who is waiting for a loan request to arrive before they pay attention has already missed the point.

The Business Has Its Own Financial Life

One of the most important adjustments a retail banker makes when moving into commercial lending is learning to read a business's financial life as distinct from the owner's personal financial life and then understanding how the two connect.

A consumer borrower's financial picture is relatively contained. Income from employment, personal debt obligations, a credit history, maybe some investment accounts. The picture fits on a few pages.

A business's financial life is more complex and more dynamic. It has revenue that fluctuates. It has expenses that are partly fixed and partly variable. It has assets, equipment, inventory, receivables, real estate, and liabilities, loans, lines of credit, accounts payable, and deferred revenue. It has a profit and loss statement that tells you what happened over time, and a balance sheet that tells you where things stand right now. And it has cash flow, which, as you'll learn in Part Two, is the most important number of all.

The Loan Is a Bet on Cash Flow

In consumer lending, the primary question is: *can this person afford the payment?* The answer is derived largely from income, existing obligations, and credit history.

In commercial lending, the primary question is different: *will this business generate enough cash flow to repay this loan?*

Not income. Not profit. Cash flow.

This is a distinction that will be developed fully in Chapter 6, but it needs to be introduced here because it is the single most important reorientation a retail banker must make. A business can be profitable on paper and still fail to repay its loans. A business can show strong revenue and still run out of cash at exactly the wrong moment.

When a commercial lender evaluates a loan request, they are making a judgment about the future performance of a business. They are asking whether the business, based on its history, its industry, its management, its market position, and its financial structure, is likely to generate enough cash flow, consistently enough, to repay the loan being requested.

These are not consumer lending questions. They are commercial lending questions. And they are the reason the business borrower requires a completely different framework than the consumer borrower does.

The Relationship Is the Context for Everything

Before we move into the mechanics of commercial lending in the chapters ahead, it is worth returning to something introduced at the beginning of this book, because it is easy to lose sight of when the technical content starts to arrive.

The business borrower is not a transaction. They are a relationship. And the quality of that relationship, built over time, through consistent communication, through genuine understanding of what the business is and where it's going, is what makes a commercial banker genuinely useful to the businesses they serve.

A lender who only sees a borrower when a loan is being requested is not a commercial banker. They are a loan processor with a business card. The commercial banker who is present across the full arc of the relationship, during the deposit conversations, during the lean quarters, during the planning conversations that happen before any request is formalized, is the banker who earns the right to be the institution that builds custom solutions when the time comes.

The business borrower is not a consumer. They are a partner. And the banker who understands that distinction before they ever open a financial statement will be a better lender, and a more valuable institution, than one who is simply trying to get the deal done.

> *Practitioner's Note: The first time you sit across from a business owner and realize you are evaluating not just a loan request but an entire enterprise, its history, its management, its market, its risks, and its potential, is the moment commercial banking becomes real. That moment will come. When it does, remember: your job is not to approve or decline. Your job is to understand. The decision follows from the understanding, not the other way around.*

CHAPTER 3

The Five Questions Every Commercial Lender Asks, And the One Everyone Forgets

Every commercial lender, whether they know it or not, is asking the same six questions every time they look at a deal. The questions don't always arrive in the same order. They aren't always stated out loud. But they are always present, running underneath every financial statement review, every borrower conversation, every credit memo written and every loan committee presentation delivered.

These questions have a formal name in banking education: the 5 Cs of credit. You may have encountered them in a training program or a certification course. If you have, you probably encountered them as a list, Character, Capacity, Capital, Conditions, Collateral, with a textbook definition attached to each one.

That's fine as far as it goes. But a list of definitions is not the same thing as a working framework. And the 5 Cs, as they're typically taught, leave something important out.

The sixth question, the one most training programs skip entirely, is the Guarantor. And in many deals, it is the question that changes everything.

This is the *5 Cs and a G*. Not five lenses. Six. And together, they are the complete framework a commercial lender uses to evaluate every credit request they will ever see.

How to Read This Chapter

Each of the six elements that follow is presented not as a definition but as a question, the actual question a lender is trying to answer when they apply that lens to a deal. Because that's what these are. Not categories on a checklist. Not boxes to fill in on a form. Questions that require judgment to answer.

The quality of your credit analysis is determined by the quality of the questions you ask. This framework is where those questions begin.

The First C: Character

Who is this borrower, and do I trust them?

Character is the first lens for a reason. Before a lender evaluates a single number, they are making a judgment about the person, or the people, behind the request. Are they honest? Do they understand their own business? Do they take responsibility for problems, or do they deflect them? Are they the kind of borrower who will call you when something goes wrong, or the kind who will go quiet and hope you don't notice?

These are not soft questions. They are foundational ones. A borrower with impeccable financial ratios and poor character is a greater risk than a borrower with modest financials and unimpeachable integrity. The numbers tell you what has happened. Character tells you something about what will happen, particularly when conditions get difficult, because at some point in any long credit relationship, conditions will get difficult.

Character is assessed through multiple channels. Credit history is one, not because the score is the point, but because repayment behavior over time is a reflection of how a borrower prioritizes their obligations. References and reputation matter. The way a borrower conducts themselves in a meeting matters. Whether they come prepared, whether they're transparent about problems, whether they've been straight with you about the things they knew you'd find anyway, all of it matters.

Character is also the lens through which the story test is most directly applied. Before a single financial statement is reviewed, a lender who has spent thirty minutes in a genuine conversation with a borrower has already formed a significant portion of their character assessment.

Listen carefully. What a borrower chooses to tell you, and what they choose not to, is itself a form of data.

The Second C: Capacity

Can this business actually repay the loan?

Capacity is the quantitative heart of commercial credit analysis. It is the question of whether the business generates, or will generate, sufficient cash flow to service the debt being requested, alongside all of its existing obligations.

This is where the income statement, the cash flow statement, and the concept of debt service coverage come into play. These will be developed fully in Part Two, but the core idea belongs here: capacity is not about what the business earns. It is about what the business keeps, after operating expenses, after taxes, after existing debt payments, and whether what remains is enough to repay the new loan comfortably, with margin to spare.

Comfortably. With margin to spare. Those qualifiers are deliberate. A loan that can only be repaid if everything goes exactly right is not a well-structured loan. Businesses encounter unexpected expenses, revenue shortfalls, and market disruptions. A lender who approves a credit based on a borrower's best-case scenario is not doing credit analysis. They are doing optimistic math.

Capacity analysis also requires understanding the *source* of repayment. Commercial lenders distinguish between primary and secondary repayment sources. The primary source is typically operating cash flow. The secondary source is typically collateral liquidation or a guarantor's personal resources, the backstop if the primary source fails.

The Third C: Capital

How much does the borrower have at stake?

Capital refers to the financial resources the borrower, the business and, in many cases, its owners, has invested in the enterprise. It answers the question of skin in the game. How much of their own money does the borrower have at risk in this venture?

A borrower who has invested substantially in their own business has a powerful personal incentive to protect that investment. A borrower who is asking a bank to finance a venture they themselves have barely committed to financially is a different proposition entirely.

Capital is evaluated through the balance sheet, specifically through the equity position of the business, the net worth of its owners, and the leverage ratio of the overall enterprise. A business that is heavily leveraged, carrying far more debt than equity, has limited financial cushion. When revenue softens, there is less capital to absorb the impact before the debt obligations become strained.

The Fourth C: Conditions

What is happening in the world this business operates in?

Conditions is the broadest of the six lenses. It asks the lender to step back from the specific borrower and evaluate the external environment in which the business operates, the industry, the market, the economic climate, and the specific purpose of the loan being requested.

A strong business operating in a deteriorating industry is a different credit risk than the same business operating in a growing one. A loan request that makes strategic sense in an expanding economy carries different risk in a contracting one.

Industry analysis is a core component of conditions. Every industry has its own risk profile, its cyclicality, its margin structure, its competitive dynamics, its regulatory environment, and its sensitivity to macroeconomic forces. A commercial lender who understands the industries they lend into is better equipped to evaluate the specific risks of any individual credit than one who analyzes each deal in isolation.

The specific purpose of the loan also falls under conditions. Why is this borrower asking for this money right now? Does the timing make sense? A line of credit requested to fund normal operating cycles is a different instrument than a line of credit requested to cover operating losses.

The Fifth C: Collateral

If this loan goes wrong, what do we have?

Collateral is the secondary repayment source, the assets a lender can look to for repayment if the primary repayment source, operating cash flow, fails. It is the backstop. The safety net.

This is the C that retail bankers often feel most comfortable with, because collateral is present in consumer lending too. A mortgage is secured by the home. An auto loan is secured by the vehicle. The concept translates.

What changes in commercial lending is the complexity of collateral evaluation and the discipline required to avoid over-relying on it.

Commercial collateral comes in many forms, real estate, equipment, inventory, accounts receivable, business assets, investment accounts, and more. Lenders apply discounts, called advance rates or loan-to-value ratios, to collateral values to account for the difference between what an asset is worth in normal conditions and what it can realistically be recovered for in a liquidation.

Here is the discipline that separates experienced commercial lenders from inexperienced ones: collateral is not a substitute for capacity. A loan that is justified primarily because the collateral is strong, but where the cash flow analysis is weak, is not a well-underwritten commercial credit. It is a collateral liquidation plan with a loan attached.

The G: Guarantor

Who is standing behind this loan, and what do they bring?

Here is the question most training programs skip. And it is the one that, in many commercial credits, changes the entire risk conversation.

A business entity, an LLC, a corporation, a partnership, is the legal borrower. But the business entity has no personal stake in the outcome beyond the assets it holds. It cannot be compelled to contribute additional resources. If the business fails and the collateral is insufficient to cover the outstanding debt, the entity's obligation ends where its assets end.

The guarantor bridges that gap.

A personal guarantee is a legal commitment by an individual, typically an owner or principal of the borrowing entity, to be personally responsible for the loan if the business cannot repay it. It extends the repayment obligation beyond the entity and onto the personal balance sheet of the guarantor.

The guarantor is not an afterthought. They are a core component of the credit structure, and evaluating the guarantor is as important as evaluating the business itself.

A guarantor assessment covers several dimensions. Personal financial strength, net worth, liquidity, personal income, existing personal obligations, tells you how much cushion exists behind the guarantee. Character of the guarantor matters independently of the character of the business. And the guarantor lens raises important questions about the nature of the business relationship: who owns this business, and are all significant owners providing guarantees?

The 5 Cs are essential. The G makes them complete.

Using the 5 Cs and a G: The Framework in Practice

The 5 Cs and a G are not a sequential checklist. They are a set of simultaneous lenses, each one illuminating a different dimension of the same credit, and each one interacting with the others in ways that require judgment rather than arithmetic.

A deal with strong capacity but weak character is a different risk than a deal with modest capacity and exceptional character. A loan with thin collateral but a financially strong guarantor is structured differently than one with strong collateral and a guarantor whose personal balance sheet is stretched. Conditions that are favorable today can shift over a five-year loan term in ways that change the entire risk profile.

The framework is not a formula. It is a way of organizing your thinking so that nothing important goes unasked.

And before you try to answer any of them with a number, answer them with a story.

Who is this borrower? What do they do, and how do they make money? Why are they here, and what are they asking for? Who is standing behind this loan, and why does this institution want to be in this relationship?

Tell the story first. Then let the 5 Cs and a G test it.

> *Practitioner's Note: The G is not optional. In commercial lending, the personal guarantee is not a formality or a piece of standard documentation. It is a credit decision in its own right. Before you accept a guarantee, understand what it's actually worth, not just what it says on paper. A guarantee without financial substance behind it is not a credit enhancement. It is a document. Know the difference.*

PART TWO

Reading the Numbers

Build financial literacy for the non-analyst.

In Part One, the foundation was laid. You understand why commercial banking is different from retail banking, why the business borrower requires a different framework than the consumer borrower, and how the 5 Cs and a G, including the Guarantor, form the complete lens through which every commercial credit is evaluated. You have been introduced to the discipline of Story Before Structure, and you understand why the story must hold before the analysis begins.

Now the analysis begins.

Part Two is about learning to read the financial statements that test the story, the income statement, the balance sheet, and the cash flow statement, and to extract from them the specific information that answers the commercial lender's primary question: does this business generate enough cash flow to repay this loan?

This is not an accounting course. You do not need a finance degree to read what follows. What you need is the willingness to approach a set of numbers the way a lender approaches them, not as a report card to be graded, but as a narrative to be interrogated. Every financial statement is telling a story. Your job is to figure out whether it's the same story the borrower told you.

Four chapters. Three financial statements. One question that runs through all of them.

Does the cash flow support the credit?

CHAPTER 4

What the Income Statement Is Really Telling You

Most people who haven't spent time in commercial banking think the income statement is the most important financial statement a business produces. It has the revenue number on it. It shows whether the business is profitable. It looks like a report card, and report cards, most of us were taught, tell you how well you're doing.

Commercial lenders know better.

The income statement is important. It is one of three financial statements you will read on every commercial credit, and it contains information that is essential to understanding the business. But it is also the most easily misread of the three, because it measures what a business*earned*, not what it *kept*. And in commercial lending, what a business keeps is the only number that matters for repayment.

The Basic Structure

The income statement, also called the profit and loss statement, or P&L, follows a consistent logical structure regardless of the size or type of business. Revenue comes in. Expenses go out. What remains is the bottom line.

Revenue is the total amount a business generates from its primary operations before any expenses are deducted. Revenue tells you the scale of the business. It does not tell you how efficiently it converts that activity into profit, or whether any of it is actually collectible.

Cost of Goods Sold, or COGS, represents the direct costs of producing whatever the business sells. Subtracting COGS from revenue produces*gross profit*, the amount the business retains after covering the direct cost of its revenue.

Operating Expenses are the costs of running the business that are not directly tied to production, rent, utilities, salaries for non-production staff, marketing, insurance, professional fees, depreciation. Subtracting operating expenses from gross profit produces*operating income*, also called EBIT, earnings before interest and taxes.

Interest Expense reflects the cost of the business's existing debt. It is separated from operating expenses because a lender needs to understand business performance independent of its current capital structure.

Taxes reflect the business's income tax obligation. For pass-through entities like S-corporations and LLCs, this line may be minimal or absent at the business level.

What remains after subtracting interest and taxes is*net income*, the bottom line. This is where most people stop reading. Commercial lenders are just getting started.

Revenue Is the Beginning, Not the Answer

Revenue is the first number on the income statement and often the first number a borrower mentions when describing their business. But revenue without context is not analysis. It is a headline.

How is revenue recognized? Some businesses recognize revenue when a contract is signed, others when work is performed, others when cash is actually received. The accounting method matters, because revenue that has been recognized but not yet collected is not the same as revenue sitting in the bank.

How concentrated is the revenue? A business generating four million dollars in annual revenue from a single customer is a fundamentally different credit risk than one generating the same revenue from four hundred customers. Concentration risk is one of the most important and most underanalyzed risks in commercial lending.

How recurring is the revenue? A business with long-term contracts or subscription-based revenue has a more predictable cash flow profile than one dependent on project-based or transactional revenue.

Is the revenue growing, stable, or declining, and why? Three years of revenue trending in one direction tells a story. A lender who accepts a single year of revenue without asking about the trend is working with incomplete information.

The Lines Between Revenue and Profit

Gross margin, gross profit divided by revenue, tells you how much the business retains after covering its direct production costs. Gross margin varies significantly by industry. What matters for credit analysis is whether the gross margin is consistent over time and consistent with industry norms.

Operating margin, operating income divided by revenue, tells you how much the business retains after both direct costs and overhead. A business with strong gross margins and weak operating margins is spending heavily on overhead relative to its revenue.

EBITDA: The Number Lenders Actually Use

If you spend time around commercial lenders, you will quickly encounter a number that doesn't appear anywhere on a standard income statement: EBITDA, Earnings Before Interest, Taxes, Depreciation, and Amortization.

EBITDA is not an accounting measure. It is an analytical tool, a way of normalizing the income statement to evaluate the operating performance of a business independent of its capital structure, tax situation, and non-cash accounting adjustments.

Interest is added back because it reflects the cost of existing debt, which may change if the loan being evaluated is approved. *Taxes* are added back because tax obligations vary based on entity structure and tax planning. *Depreciation and amortization* are added back because they are non-cash expenses, they reduced reported net income without consuming actual cash.

EBITDA is a starting point, not an ending point. It overstates available cash flow because it ignores capital expenditure, the actual cash spent to maintain and replace the physical assets whose depreciation was just added back.

Net Operating Income and the Line That Matters Most

For commercial real estate loans, and for many operating businesses with significant fixed asset bases, lenders use a related measure called *Net Operating Income*, or NOI.

NOI is calculated by taking gross revenue and subtracting operating expenses, but before debt service. It represents what the property or business generates from its operations before the cost of financing is deducted.

NOI is the most direct measure of a business's ability to service debt, because debt service is what you're measuring against it. The ratio of NOI to annual debt service requirements is the *Debt Service Coverage Ratio*, or DSCR, the single most important metric in commercial lending.

What the Income Statement Doesn't Tell You

The income statement is an accrual document. It records revenue when it is earned, and expenses when they are incurred, regardless of when cash actually changes hands. A business can record a million dollars in revenue in December and not collect a dollar of it until March.

This is why the income statement alone is insufficient for commercial credit analysis. It must be read alongside the balance sheet, which shows what the business owns and owes at a point in time, and the cash flow statement, which shows the actual movement of cash.

Of the three, the cash flow statement is the one that most directly answers the commercial lender's primary question. We will get there in Chapter 6. But before that, we need to understand the balance sheet, because it is the document that tells you whether the foundation the business is standing on is solid or cracked.

Reading the Income Statement as a Story

A commercial lender who has read this chapter carefully will approach an income statement as a narrative to be interrogated. Where does the revenue come from, and how reliable is it? What does the margin structure tell you? What does the trend over three years tell you that a single year does not? What is EBITDA, and what does it say about the business's capacity to service debt?

The borrower told you a story in your first conversation. The income statement is telling you another one. Your job is to figure out whether they're the same story.

> *Practitioner's Note: Always ask for three years of income statements, not one. A single year tells you where a business is. Three years tell you where it's been, how it handles pressure, and whether the performance you're seeing is a trend or an anomaly. A borrower who is reluctant to provide three years of financials is a borrower who is asking you to make a credit decision with incomplete information. That reluctance is itself a data point.*

CHAPTER 5

The Balance Sheet as a Risk Map

The income statement tells you how a business performed over a period of time. The balance sheet tells you where it stands right now.

Think of the balance sheet as a photograph taken on a specific date. Everything the business owns is on one side. Everything it owes is on the other. What remains after subtracting what it owes from what it owns is the equity, the net worth of the enterprise. That photograph, read carefully, reveals the financial architecture of the business. Its strengths, its vulnerabilities, the weight it's carrying, and whether the foundation it's standing on can support the additional load of the loan being requested.

The Basic Structure

The balance sheet is organized around a simple equation that has governed accounting for centuries:

Assets = Liabilities + Equity

Everything a business owns was financed by someone, either by creditors, who provided debt, or by owners, who provided equity. The left side is what the business has. The right side is who paid for it.

Assets: What the Business Has

Current assets are assets expected to be converted to cash, sold, or consumed within the next twelve months. They include:

Cash and cash equivalents - the most liquid asset on the balance sheet. Cash is the lifeblood of a business, and a lender who ignores the cash balance, its level, its trend, and its seasonality, is missing one of the most direct signals of financial health.

Accounts receivable - money owed to the business by its customers for goods delivered or services rendered but not yet collected. The quality of a business's receivables, how old they are, how concentrated they are, and how reliably they are collected, is a significant credit consideration. An aging receivables schedule is one of the most useful documents a commercial lender can request.

Inventory - the goods a business holds for sale or for use in production. The quality of inventory matters as much as the quantity. Lenders apply meaningful discounts to inventory values when evaluating collateral.

Non-current assets are assets not expected to be converted to cash within twelve months, the longer-term infrastructure of the business.

Property, plant, and equipment (PP&E) - includes land, buildings, machinery, vehicles, and other physical assets used in operations. The net value on the balance sheet, cost minus accumulated depreciation, is the book value of the asset, which may or may not reflect its actual market value.

Intangible assets - include patents, trademarks, customer lists, non-compete agreements, and goodwill. Goodwill in particular is treated cautiously in credit analysis, it has no liquidation value and cannot be sold independently.

Liabilities: What the Business Owes

Current liabilities are obligations due within the next twelve months, including accounts payable, accrued liabilities, and short-term debt.

Accounts payable - money the business owes to its suppliers. A business that is stretching its payables, paying suppliers more slowly than normal, may be managing a cash flow problem not yet visible in the income statement.

Non-current liabilities are obligations not due within the next twelve months, the longer-term debt structure of the business. A commercial lender evaluating a new loan needs to understand the full existing debt load, its maturity schedule, interest rates, covenants, and the collateral already pledged to other lenders.

Equity: What Belongs to the Owners

Equity is the residual interest in the business after all liabilities have been subtracted from all assets. It represents the owners' stake, the accumulated investment and retained earnings.

Retained earnings, the cumulative net income a business has generated over its history, minus any distributions paid to owners, are one of the most telling lines on the balance sheet. A business with strong retained earnings has been consistently profitable over time. A business with negative retained earnings has lost more than it has made or distributed more than it has earned.

The Relationship Between Assets and Liabilities: Reading Leverage

Leverage is the degree to which a business has used debt to finance its assets. A highly leveraged business has borrowed heavily against a thin equity base.

Equity is a cushion. When a business encounters difficulty, the equity cushion absorbs the impact before creditors are affected. The thicker the cushion, the more stress the business can absorb. The thinner the cushion, the less runway it has.

The *debt-to-equity ratio* compares total liabilities to total equity. The *debt-to-assets ratio* compares total liabilities to total assets, answering what percentage of the business's assets are financed by debt.

Working Capital: The Operational Pulse

Working capital, current assets minus current liabilities, measures the liquidity available to fund the business's day-to-day operations. The *current ratio*, current assets divided by current liabilities, expresses this as a ratio.

Understanding the seasonality of the business and what the working capital position looks like across the full cycle, not just at the balance sheet date, is essential to reading this metric accurately.

The Balance Sheet and the Guarantor

The guarantor's personal balance sheet is evaluated with exactly the same discipline as the business balance sheet. What does the guarantor own? What do they owe? What is their personal net worth, and how much of it is liquid, and how much is tied up in the same business being financed?

A guarantor whose personal net worth is almost entirely represented by their equity in the business being financed is not providing the independent secondary repayment source that a guarantee is intended to represent. This is why the personal financial statement is not a formality. It is a balance sheet in its own right, and it deserves the same careful reading.

Reading the Balance Sheet as a Risk Map

The asset side shows what the business has built. The liability side shows the claims against those resources. The equity tells you how much cushion exists between the business's assets and its creditors' claims, and whether that cushion has been growing or eroding over time.

The income statement told you what the business earned. The balance sheet tells you where it stands. The next chapter will complete the picture, because neither will tell you the one thing a commercial lender needs to know most of all. Whether the business actually generates cash.

> *Practitioner's Note: Always ask for balance sheets dated at the same point across multiple years, ideally year-end for at least three consecutive years. A balance sheet is a snapshot, and a single snapshot can be misleading. Three snapshots taken at the same point in the business's annual cycle will show you the trend, whether equity is building or eroding, whether leverage is increasing or decreasing. Trend is almost always more instructive than a single data point.*

CHAPTER 6

Cash Flow Is Not Profit

If there is one sentence in this book worth underlining, writing on a notecard, and taping to your monitor in the first year of your commercial lending career, it is this:

A business can be profitable and still fail to repay its loans.

Not because the owners are dishonest. Not because the financials were fabricated. But because profit and cash flow are not the same thing, and in commercial lending, cash flow is the only currency that actually repays debt.

Why Profit and Cash Flow Diverge

The income statement is built on accrual accounting. Accrual accounting records revenue when it is earned and expenses when they are incurred, regardless of when cash actually changes hands.

For a commercial lender evaluating whether a business can repay its debt, accrual accounting creates a problem. A business reports two million dollars in revenue and one million dollars in net income. But if four hundred thousand dollars of that revenue hasn't been collected yet, the actual cash generated is closer to six hundred thousand dollars. Profit said one million. Cash said six hundred thousand.

The Four Places Profit Goes Without Becoming Cash

Accounts receivable growth. When a business grows its revenue, it typically grows its receivables along with it. Each dollar of revenue that hasn't been collected yet is a dollar of profit that hasn't become cash. If receivables are growing faster than the business is collecting them, the income statement can show strong earnings while the bank account is being quietly drained.

Inventory buildup. For businesses that carry inventory, purchasing inventory requires cash before any revenue is generated. A business can be growing profitably and running out of cash simultaneously, a condition sometimes called overtrading, because its working capital needs are outpacing its cash generation.

Capital expenditures. When a business buys equipment or other fixed assets, it spends cash. But the income statement reflects only the depreciation of the asset over time, not the cash outflow. This is one of the reasons EBITDA can overstate available cash flow for capital-intensive businesses.

Debt repayment. Principal payments on existing loans do not flow through the income statement. Interest payments do. But the principal portion of each loan payment reduces cash without touching the income statement, which is why net income is an incomplete measure of debt service capacity.

The Cash Flow Statement

The cash flow statement bridges the gap between profit and cash. It is organized into three sections.

Cash flow from operations is the most important section for commercial credit analysis. It starts with net income and adjusts for non-cash expenses and working capital changes, producing a measure of the actual cash the business generated from its core operations during the period.

Cash flow from investing reflects the cash the business spent on or received from capital expenditures, asset sales, and investments. This is where the actual cash cost of fixed asset purchases appears, the number that EBITDA obscures.

Cash flow from financing reflects cash flows related to the business's debt and equity structure, loan proceeds received, principal payments made, equity contributions, and owner distributions.

Free Cash Flow: What's Actually Left

Free cash flow, operating cash flow minus capital expenditures required to maintain the business's existing productive capacity, is the most honest measure of debt service capacity. It accounts for the actual cash demands of the business before any debt payments are considered.

Free Cash Flow = Operating Cash Flow − Maintenance Capital Expenditures

Debt Service Coverage Ratio: The Number That Matters Most

With free cash flow established, a commercial lender can calculate the single most important metric in commercial credit analysis: the *Debt Service Coverage Ratio*, or DSCR.

DSCR = Net Operating Income (or Free Cash Flow) ÷ Total Annual Debt Service

Total annual debt service is the sum of all principal and interest payments the business is required to make in a given year, on all of its debt obligations, including the proposed new loan.

A DSCR of 1.25 means the business generates $1.25 in cash flow for every $1.00 of debt service, a twenty-five percent cushion above the minimum required. A DSCR of 1.00 means the business is generating exactly enough to cover its debt service, no cushion, no margin for error. A DSCR below 1.00 means the business cannot cover its debt service from operations.

Most commercial lenders require a minimum DSCR of 1.20 to 1.25 for standard commercial credits. The threshold represents a judgment about how much cushion is required to absorb normal business variability without impairing the institution's ability to be repaid.

Cash Flow and the Story

The cash flow story of a business is not just a number. It is a narrative about how the business converts its commercial activity into actual, available cash, and how reliably it does so over time, across conditions, and under pressure.

When you sit across from a borrower and ask them to tell you about their business, you are, among other things, listening for the cash flow story. How does the business get paid? How quickly? What happens to cash flow in a slow month? A borrower who can answer those questions clearly understands their own cash flow. A borrower who can't is telling you something important.

Cash flow is not profit. It is the truth underneath the profit. And in commercial lending, the truth is the only thing that repays a loan.

A Practical Summary

The income statement tells you what the business earned, but earnings are an accrual concept. The cash flow statement tells you what the business actually generated and spent in cash. Free cash flow, operating cash flow minus capital expenditures, is what remains after the business has maintained its productive capacity. DSCR measures how many times that pool covers the total annual debt service obligation. A DSCR above 1.25 provides meaningful cushion. A DSCR at or below 1.00 means the business is not self-funding its debt.

> *Practitioner's Note: When a borrower tells you the business is profitable, your next question should always be: "Walk me through how the business generates cash." Profit is reported. Cash is real. A borrower who understands their own cash flow cycle,*

who can explain the timing between revenue, collections, expenses, and available cash without hesitation, is demonstrating exactly the kind of financial management competence that a commercial lender wants to see.

CHAPTER 7

Collateral: The Second Way Out

There is a saying that has circulated among commercial lenders for as long as commercial lending has existed: *a good loan doesn't need collateral, and collateral doesn't make a bad loan good.*

Every experienced lender knows this. And yet collateral remains one of the most misunderstood and most misused concepts in commercial credit. It gets over-relied on when cash flow analysis is weak. It gets treated as a substitute for underwriting when the story doesn't quite hold together.

What Collateral Is

Collateral is the secondary repayment source. It is the assets a lender can look to for repayment if the primary repayment source, operating cash flow, fails to perform as expected.

The word *secondary* is not incidental. It carries the entire weight of the concept. Collateral is not the first way a loan gets repaid. It is the second way. When collateral is treated as the primary story rather than the secondary one, the credit structure has been inverted. The lender is no longer making a business loan. They are making a liquidation plan with a loan attached.

Why Collateral Matters

Even when cash flow analysis is strong, collateral serves important functions. It aligns incentives, a borrower who has pledged meaningful assets has a direct personal stake in the performance of the loan. It provides a recovery mechanism when loans fail despite sound original underwriting. And it informs structure, the type and quality of available collateral often influences how a loan should be built.

Types of Commercial Collateral

Real estate is the most common and generally the most reliable form of commercial collateral. Commercial real estate can be valued with reasonable precision through a formal appraisal, and lenders apply a loan-to-value ratio to determine the maximum loan amount the collateral will support.

Equipment is a common form of collateral for manufacturers, contractors, and transportation companies. The central challenge is depreciation, both accounting depreciation and actual market value deterioration. Lenders advance against equipment at rates reflecting liquidation reality, typically fifty to seventy percent of orderly liquidation value.

Accounts receivable represent money owed to the business by its customers. Receivable quality varies significantly. Lenders evaluate receivables through an aging analysis, applying advance rates to eligible receivables and excluding concentrations and aged balances.

Inventory is among the most complex and most carefully discounted forms of commercial collateral. Lenders advance against inventory at rates that reflect liquidation risk, often twenty-five to fifty percent of stated inventory value.

Cash and liquid investments are the most straightforward form of collateral. A loan secured by a certificate of deposit is essentially a risk-free credit, which is why advance rates against cash collateral are typically one hundred percent.

Personal assets, the primary residence, investment accounts, personal real estate, are frequently pledged as collateral in smaller commercial transactions. Personal collateral is evaluated with the same rigor as business collateral.

How Collateral Is Valued: The Gap Between Book and Reality

Fair market value is the price at which an asset would change hands between a willing buyer and a willing seller, neither under compulsion. This is the standard appraisal value.

Orderly liquidation value is lower, the estimated proceeds achievable in a liquidation conducted over a reasonable period of time. This is the benchmark most commercial lenders use for equipment and inventory collateral.

Forced liquidation value is lower still, the estimated proceeds in a rapid, time-pressured sale. Forced liquidation values can be dramatically lower than fair market values, particularly for specialized assets.

The UCC Filing and the Perfected Security Interest

For most types of personal property collateral, perfection is accomplished through a *UCC-1 financing statement* filed with the appropriate state authority. The UCC-1 filing is a public notice that the lender has a security interest in the described collateral. It establishes the lender's priority claim against that collateral relative to other creditors.

Priority matters enormously in a default scenario. A first-priority lien holder has the first claim on collateral proceeds. A second-priority lien holder receives what remains after the first-priority claim is satisfied. A lender who takes collateral without perfecting their security interest has not actually secured that collateral.

Collateral and the Guarantor: The Full Secondary Picture

Collateral and the guarantor together constitute the secondary repayment picture. Neither should be evaluated in isolation. A loan with strong collateral and a weak guarantor has asset protection but limited personal commitment. A loan with a strong guarantor and modest collateral has personal commitment but limited asset recovery. The complete secondary picture requires both.

The Discipline: Collateral as a Complement, Never a Substitute

Everything in this chapter leads back to the principle stated at its beginning: collateral is the second way out. Not the first. Not the primary justification for a credit approval. The backstop.

The best commercial lenders approach collateral with a specific discipline: underwrite the loan as though the collateral doesn't exist. Build the credit case on cash flow, capacity, character, and the full strength of the 5 Cs and a G. Then confirm that the collateral is there, properly valued, properly secured, and sufficient to provide meaningful protection if the primary repayment source fails.

That sequence, cash flow first, collateral second, is not just a philosophical preference. It is the practice that distinguishes sound commercial lending from secured asset management.

> *Practitioner's Note: The most dangerous words in commercial lending are "we're well-collateralized." They are dangerous not because they are false, sometimes they are entirely accurate, but because of what they are used to justify. A well-collateralized loan with weak cash flow is not a safe loan. It is a loan where the exit strategy is default and recovery rather than repayment. Before those words close a credit discussion, ask one more question: what does the actual liquidation process look like, and what will we realistically net after costs, time, and market conditions?*

PART THREE

How a Deal Comes Together

Walk the reader through the lending lifecycle.

Parts One and Two built the foundation. You understand the mindset shift the move into commercial banking requires. You can read a financial statement not as a scorecard but as a story, identifying the cash flow behind the profit, the risk map behind the balance sheet, and the collateral discipline that separates a genuine secondary repayment source from a liquidation plan with a loan attached. You know the 5 Cs and a G. You know what cash flow is and what it isn't. You know what collateral can and cannot do.

Now the deal comes together.

Part Three is about the full arc of the commercial credit relationship, from the moment a loan request arrives on your desk to the structure that is built around it to the mindset a commercial banker carries into every conversation, every credit decision, and every relationship across a career.

Chapter 8 is about the loan request, what it is, how to read it, how to tell the story that makes it presentable, and how to know whether the institution you work for is positioned to act on it. Chapter 9 is about structure, how to match the loan to its purpose, how to build custom rather than select from a shelf, and how to have the rate and fee conversation with a borrower in a way that builds trust rather than friction. Chapter 10 is about the lender's mindset, the orientation that holds all of it together, from the first deposit conversation to the last payment on the last loan in a decades-long relationship.

The foundation is laid. The analysis is done. The deal is in front of you. Let's build it.

CHAPTER 8

The Loan Request: What You're Really Being Asked to Evaluate

A loan request arrives in many forms. Sometimes it's a formal application with a package of financial statements, tax returns, and supporting documentation already assembled. Sometimes it's a phone call from a business owner who heard you work with companies like theirs. Sometimes it's a conversation that starts about a checking account and ends with a question about whether you'd be interested in taking a look at a financing need.

Regardless of how it arrives, a loan request is always the same thing at its core: an invitation to evaluate a relationship.

Before You Open the File

The first mistake most new commercial bankers make when a loan request arrives is reaching for the financial statements. The financials feel like the objective part. But before you open a financial statement, before you pull a credit report, before you calculate a single ratio, you need to be able to tell the story.

A lender who runs the numbers first and builds the story around them afterward is working in the wrong direction. They are at risk of constructing a narrative to justify what the numbers appear to support, rather than using the numbers to test a narrative they already understand.

The Story Test

Before any formal analysis begins, a commercial lender should be able to answer six questions in plain language, without a spreadsheet open, without a financial statement in front of them, and without hesitation.

Who is this borrower? Not their legal entity name. Who are they, the people behind the business? How long have they been in this industry? What do you know about their character and reputation?

What does this business do, and how does it actually make money? Not the industry category. The actual operating model, what the business sells, who it sells to, how it gets paid, and what the relationship between its revenue and its cash looks like in practice.

Why are they here, and what are they asking for? The specific request, amount, structure, purpose, and the reason it's being made now. Does the timing make sense?

Why does this request make sense for the business? Not just that the borrower wants it, but that it is strategically and financially logical. Does the purpose align with the business's actual needs?

Why does this relationship make sense for your institution? This is the question most training programs don't ask. Not every creditworthy loan request is the right loan for your institution. Does this deal fit your institution's risk appetite, industry concentrations, and relationship objectives?

Who is standing behind this loan, and why does that matter? The guarantor belongs in the story before it belongs in the credit memo.

What a Loan Request Is Really Made Of

A loan request is a layered communication, and each layer contains information a commercial lender needs to extract and evaluate.

The stated request is the surface layer. Amount, purpose, proposed term, proposed structure. Pay attention to whether the stated request makes internal sense. Is the amount consistent with the stated purpose? Is the proposed structure consistent with the asset or activity being financed?

The underlying need is the layer beneath the stated request. What problem is the borrower actually trying to solve? Sometimes the stated request and the underlying need are the same thing. Often they are not.

The relationship context is the layer beneath the underlying need. What is the history between this borrower and your institution? Why are they here, at this institution, making this request now?

Reading the Borrower's Narrative

Several dimensions of the narrative deserve specific attention.

Ownership and transparency. Does the borrower acknowledge challenges in their business, or do they present only the favorable picture? A business owner who proactively identifies the risks in their own request is demonstrating a level of transparency that is itself a character indicator.

Depth of understanding. Does the borrower understand their own business at a financial level? Can they explain their revenue model, their margin structure, their cash flow cycle without prompting?

Consistency. Does the narrative the borrower presents verbally match what the financial statements say? Any material inconsistency warrants a direct and respectful clarifying question.

The ask itself. A borrower who has thought carefully about the amount they need, the structure that makes sense, and the repayment source is demonstrating financial discipline.

What's Missing Is as Important as What's There

What hasn't the borrower mentioned? What question has been answered vaguely when it should have been answered precisely? Missing information is not always evidence of concealment. But it always represents an open question, and open questions are the lender's responsibility to close before the analysis is complete.

The completeness of the information a borrower provides, and the attitude with which they provide it, is a character indicator. Treat it as one.

The Difference Between a Deal and a Relationship

A deal is a transaction, it has a closing date, a maturity date, and a defined repayment schedule. A relationship is an ongoing financial partnership that evolves as the business grows and changes.

The best commercial bankers hold both evaluations simultaneously. They ask whether this specific credit makes sense on its own terms. And they ask whether this borrower, in this business, at this stage of their growth, is the kind of relationship their institution wants to build.

Sometimes the answer to the first question is yes and the second is no. Sometimes the answer to the first is not quite yet but the second is yes. This is judgment, it cannot be automated or outsourced to a credit scoring model.

Right Deal, Wrong Institution

There is a conversation that happens regularly in commercial banking, and it almost never appears in a training program.

A banker brings a deal forward. The story is clean. The financials are solid. The borrower is credible, the collateral is adequate, and the DSCR clears the minimum threshold with meaningful cushion. The 5 Cs and a G all check out. By every measure the banker has been taught to apply, this is an approvable credit. And the institution passes on it.

Not because the deal is bad. Not because the banker made an analytical error. Not because the borrower did anything wrong. But because the institution, at this moment, for its own reasons, is not the right home for this particular credit.

This is called institutional appetite. And understanding it is one of the most important, and most underteached, dimensions of commercial banking.

What Institutional Appetite Is

Every bank and credit union has a set of relationship types, industries, loan structures, and borrower profiles it is willing to pursue at any given point in time. Some of these preferences are explicit, written into a credit policy, a concentration limit, or a strategic plan. Others are implicit, shaped by recent experience, portfolio performance, regulatory feedback, or the quiet consensus of a leadership team that has decided, for now, to move in a different direction.

This is institutional appetite. It is not a fixed list. It is a living, shifting expression of what the institution is positioned, and willing, to do right now.

What Drives Appetite

Portfolio concentration. When a specific category approaches its concentration limit, the institution's appetite for additional credits in that category diminishes, regardless of individual deal quality.

Recent credit losses. When an institution experiences significant losses in a specific industry or loan type, appetite for that category contracts. Sometimes formally through revised credit policy. Sometimes informally through quiet institutional skepticism.

Regulatory examination findings. An institution that received criticism in its most recent examination about a specific loan type will have reduced appetite for that category until the concerns have been addressed.

Expertise and ongoing management capability. Some loan types require specialized underwriting expertise and monitoring capability that not every institution has developed. An institution that lacks the internal expertise to properly underwrite and manage a specific loan type should not have appetite for it.

Strategic direction. Institutions periodically reassess their strategic priorities. A deal that doesn't fit that strategic direction is a deal without a home at that institution, even if its financial profile is excellent.

How Appetite Changes

Institutional appetite is not static. It shifts, sometimes gradually, as strategic priorities evolve, and sometimes quickly, in response to an examination finding, a significant credit loss, or a change in leadership.

A banker who calibrated their institution's appetite eighteen months ago and hasn't updated that calibration is working from a map that may no longer reflect the territory. The practical implication: institutional appetite requires ongoing attention, direct communication with the chief credit officer, the senior lender, the lending committee. Ask regularly, not just when a specific deal is in front of you.

What It Means for the Banker

The discipline of knowing your institution's appetite before you begin a credit conversation is one of the most practically valuable habits a commercial banker can develop. A banker who starts a credit conversation on a relationship type the institution isn't positioned to do has created two problems: a disappointed borrower who shared their financial picture and invested time, and a damaged relationship.

If the answer is yes, proceed with the full discipline this chapter has described. If the answer is no, or not right now, have that conversation honestly and early. The honest conversation is not a relationship-ending one. A banker who tells the truth early, and who occasionally refers a borrower to a better-positioned institution, earns a level of trust that the deal-at-any-cost banker never will.

What It Means for the Credit Decision

The question is never just: is this a good deal? The question is: is this a good deal for this institution, right now? Those are different questions. And a commercial banker who understands the difference will bring better deals, have better conversations, and build a stronger portfolio than one who treats institutional appetite as an obstacle rather than a legitimate dimension of sound commercial banking.

Preparing to Present

Every loan request that moves forward past the initial evaluation eventually requires a presentation, to a credit officer, a loan committee, or a senior lender. The foundation of every credit presentation is the story, stated clearly, completely, and in the order that makes it easiest to follow.

A credit presentation that leads with the numbers before the story has been told asks the reader to evaluate data without context. A credit presentation that omits the risks is not a credit presentation. It is a sales pitch. Senior lenders and credit officers have seen enough files to find what wasn't disclosed. A banker whose presentations consistently omit inconvenient information will lose the trust of the people they present to.

Present the full picture. Lead with the story. Let the analysis test the story. Disclose the risks and explain how the structure addresses them. State your recommendation clearly and be prepared to defend it. That is the job.

Story Before Structure: The Test

At the end of every initial loan request review, before the credit memo is drafted, there is a simple test worth applying.

Can you tell the story of this deal, out loud, in plain language, to someone who has not seen the file, and have it make sense? Not the ratios. Not the advance rates. Not the covenant structure. The story.

Who is this borrower, what do they do, why are they asking for this, why does it make sense for them, why does it make sense for your institution, and who is standing behind it?

If the story holds together, clear, consistent, internally logical, and supported by the financial analysis, you are ready to move forward. If it doesn't, if there are gaps, inconsistencies, or questions you've been avoiding, you are not ready. You are ready to go back and ask the questions you haven't asked yet.

Story Before Structure is not a slogan. It is a discipline. And it is the discipline that, applied consistently, will make you a better commercial banker than any ratio or formula ever could.

> *Practitioner's Note: The most common failure point in commercial credit is not analytical error, it is the decision to move forward before the story is fully understood. A banker under pressure to book a loan, meet a production goal, or satisfy a borrower who is growing impatient will sometimes advance a credit before the open questions are closed. That pressure is real. The discipline required to resist it, to hold the story to the same standard regardless of external pressure, is one of the defining characteristics of a lender whose portfolio performs well over time.*

CHAPTER 9

Structure Basics: Matching the Loan to the Purpose

A loan is not just a number and an interest rate. It is a structure, a carefully designed set of terms, conditions, and constraints that defines how capital is deployed, how it is repaid, and what protections exist for the institution over the life of the credit relationship.

Structure is where the analysis becomes the deal. Everything in the previous chapters, the story, the financial analysis, the 5 Cs and a G, the cash flow evaluation, the collateral assessment, flows into a single practical question: given what we know about this borrower, this business, and this request, how should this loan be built?

An incorrectly structured loan mismatches repayment obligations with cash flow timing, funds long-term needs with short-term instruments or vice versa, and leaves the institution without the information or contractual tools to respond when the credit deteriorates.

The Freedom and the Responsibility of Custom Built

Before the building blocks of structure are introduced, one principle deserves to be stated plainly, because it reframes everything that follows.

In commercial banking, there is no shelf. There are principles, frameworks, and conventions, and they exist for good reasons, because experience has shown what works for specific types of borrowing needs. But within those principles, the range of what can be built is remarkably wide.

If a banker can understand the business well enough to identify what it actually needs, analyze the risk well enough to quantify it honestly, and build a structure that serves the borrower's purpose while protecting the institution's position, that structure can be built.

This is the freedom of commercial banking. And it comes with an equally important constraint: the structure must work for both parties. A loan that serves the borrower's immediate need but exposes the institution to risk it cannot properly evaluate, monitor, or manage is not a well-built loan. The standard is mutual benefit, and mutual benefit requires a banker who understands both sides of the equation.

Custom built means something specific. It means the structure was designed around the specific needs and risk profile of this borrower, this business, and this purpose. Not selected from a menu. Not approximated from a template. Designed. And the freedom to design is what makes getting the design right so important.

Structure is not paperwork. It is risk management expressed in contractual form.

The Foundational Question: What Is the Money For?

Every structural decision in a commercial loan begins with a single foundational question: what is the money for? The purpose of the loan determines virtually every element of its structure.

Working capital, the cash needed to fund the operating cycle between when the business spends and when it collects. The appropriate structure is a revolving line of credit.

Asset acquisition, the purchase of equipment, vehicles, or other fixed assets. The appropriate structure is a term loan with a defined amortization schedule tied to the useful life of the asset.

Real estate, the purchase or refinancing of commercial property. Real estate loans carry longer terms, formal appraisal requirements, and loan-to-value structures.

Growth and acquisition, financing business expansion or the acquisition of another business. Varies in structure depending on the nature of the growth.

Term Loans

A term loan is a fixed advance of capital repaid over a defined period through scheduled payments of principal and interest. It is the foundational instrument of commercial lending.

Principal amount is the total amount advanced at closing. Unlike a revolving line, a term loan is typically funded in a single advance. *Term* is the total life of the loan. *Amortization* is the schedule by which principal is repaid. A fully amortizing loan reaches zero balance at maturity. A partially amortizing loan, sometimes called a balloon loan, leaves a lump sum due at maturity.

Interest rate may be fixed or variable. Fixed rates provide certainty to the borrower. Variable rates transfer interest rate risk to the borrower. A borrower whose cash flow is tight relative to debt service requirements is more vulnerable to rate increases under a variable structure.

Lines of Credit

A revolving line of credit is a commitment by the institution to advance funds up to a specified maximum, on a revolving basis, as the borrower's needs require.

Annual cleanup, also called the resting period, is a structural requirement that the line of credit be paid to zero, or near zero, for a period of time each year, typically thirty consecutive days. The cleanup, or rest, confirms that the business can operate without the line for a period, that the line is supplementing cash flow rather than replacing it. A business that cannot achieve annual cleanup is telling you something important about its actual liquidity position.

Borrowing base ties the maximum available amount to the value of specific current assets, typically eligible accounts receivable and eligible inventory. *Commitment period* is the term of the line, typically one year, subject to annual review and renewal.

Matching Structure to Purpose: The Mismatch Problem

Long-term need funded with short-term debt creates refinancing risk. A business using a one-year line to purchase equipment creates a situation where the debt matures long before the asset generates the cash flow needed to repay it.

Short-term need funded with long-term debt obscures credit quality. A business converting a working capital shortfall into a five-year term loan has solved a short-term problem with a long-term obligation. The underlying problem will resurface.

Structure mismatch is a risk signal. When the proposed structure doesn't fit the purpose, ask whether the mismatch is a structuring error or a credit signal. A borrower requesting a term loan for what is clearly a working capital need may be unable to qualify for a revolving line.

Covenants: Structure as Ongoing Risk Management

A loan covenant is a contractual commitment the borrower makes to the institution as a condition of the loan. Covenants are monitoring mechanisms, tools that allow the institution to track the financial health of the borrower and act before a deteriorating credit becomes a non-performing one.

Affirmative covenants require the borrower to do specific things, provide annual financial statements, maintain adequate insurance, pay taxes on time. *Negative covenants* prohibit the borrower from doing specific things without lender consent, taking on additional debt, selling collateral, making large distributions. *Financial covenants* establish minimum performance standards, typically minimum DSCR of 1.20x to 1.25x and maximum leverage ratios.

Covenants are only effective if they are monitored. A loan officer who collects annual financial statements and files them without testing the covenants has the form of monitoring without its substance.

Guarantees as Structure

The personal guarantee is a structural element of the loan, the contractual mechanism by which the institution extends its claim beyond the entity and onto the personal balance sheet of the owner.

An*unlimited personal guarantee* obligates the guarantor for the full outstanding balance. A *limited guarantee* caps the obligation at a specified amount. A *completion guarantee*, common in construction lending, obligates the guarantor to complete the project regardless of cost. The structure of the guarantee and the financial substance behind it both belong in the credit memo.

Structure and substance must align.

The Pricing Conversation

Rate and fee, the two questions every borrower asks and every banker needs to answer well.

How Commercial Loan Rates Are Determined, And How to Talk About Them

Interest rate is one of the first questions a business borrower asks and one of the questions retail bankers converting to commercial lending are least prepared to answer. In retail banking, rates are largely standardized, posted, published, available on a rate sheet. In commercial banking, that conversation doesn't work the same way. Because the loan is custom built, so is the rate.

Every commercial loan rate is built from two components.

The Index is the starting point, a market-based benchmark rate reflecting the current cost of money. For commercial loans, the index is typically tied to the U.S. Treasury yield for the term that matches the loan being structured. A five-year term loan uses the five-year Treasury as its index. A variable rate line of credit may use the prime rate or SOFR. Treasury rates move daily based on supply and demand in the market, outside the bank's control, which is one of the reasons a commercial rate cannot be quoted with precision before the loan is ready to close.

The Margin is what the bank adds above the index, compensation for the cost of building and administering the loan, and the risk of holding it on the balance sheet over its term. The margin reflects the credit risk of the specific borrower, the structure, the collateral quality, the term, and the full value of the banking relationship.

Rate = *Index* + *Margin.* Those two numbers, added together, produce the interest rate on the loan. The index reflects the market. The margin reflects the credit.

When a business borrower asks about rates, here is the answer that works:

"Business loans are built individually, the rate is based on the design of the loan, our cost to build and carry it, the risk profile of the credit, and the overall relationship. I can't give you an exact number until we understand the full picture. What I can tell you is how it works: we start with a Treasury rate that matches the term of the loan, the index. We then add a margin above that index to reflect our cost and the risk. Those two pieces together make the rate. Treasury rates move daily, so the index isn't fixed until the loan closes. For a commercial real estate loan, we're generally seeing rates in the range of the corresponding Treasury, five-year Treasury for a five-year loan, ten-year Treasury for a longer term, plus two and a half to three and a half percent. That range will tighten once we've worked through the details together."

That answer validates the question, explains the framework, is honest about why precision isn't yet available, and gives the borrower a reference point for planning, without binding the institution to a number that may not survive the underwriting process.

Loan Fees, The Other Component of Loan Pricing

The interest rate is not the only cost of a commercial loan. Most commercial loans carry an origination fee, sometimes called a loan fee, a commitment fee, or a points charge, paid at closing as part of the cost of obtaining the financing.

A commercial loan origination fee reflects two things: the complexity of the loan being built and the depth of the relationship between the borrower and the institution.

Complexity is the work component. A straightforward owner-occupied commercial real estate loan represents a certain level of work to originate. A construction loan with multiple draw requests represents significantly more. The fee reflects the institution's cost to build, underwrite, document, and close the loan.

Relationship depth is the context component. An institution that has banked a borrower for ten years has a different cost basis for the relationship than one meeting the borrower through a single loan request. The deeper the relationship, the more the institution's overall revenue justifies a more favorable fee structure.

For a standard rate-and-term commercial loan, a straightforward term loan or commercial real estate loan with no unusual structural complexity, origination fees are generally around one percent of the loan amount. A $750,000 loan at one percent carries a fee of $7,500. That baseline moves in both directions based on complexity and relationship depth.

Fees are collected at closing, disclosed in the loan commitment letter before the borrower signs. Fees may also be financed into the loan amount, though a banker who offers to finance fees without explaining the cost implications is not serving the borrower well. A financed fee accrues interest over the life of the loan.

The Rate Is Not the Relationship

In retail banking, the rate is often the primary competitive variable. A consumer shopping for a mortgage compares rates across institutions and the rate is the primary decision variable.

In commercial banking, the rate is one component of a custom-built structure, and it is rarely the primary decision variable for a business owner building a long-term banking relationship. The commercial banker who leads with rate is competing on the wrong dimension. The commercial banker who leads with understanding, who demonstrates genuine knowledge of the business, asks the right questions, and builds a structure that actually fits, is competing on the dimension that builds lasting relationships.

The rate follows the structure. The structure follows the story. The story follows the relationship. That is the order of operations in commercial banking.

The Structure Conversation With the Borrower

Commercial loan structure is not something a lender presents to a borrower as a fait accompli. It is the outcome of a conversation, one in which the lender's structural judgment and the borrower's operational reality are brought into alignment.

A borrower who understands why their loan is structured the way it is, who understands that the amortization schedule was chosen to match the cash flow of the asset being financed, that the covenant was set to provide early warning of deterioration, is a borrower who is less likely to experience the structure as adversarial.

Structure is where custom built becomes tangible. The financial analysis identified the story. The 5 Cs and a G evaluated the risk. The structure is the answer, designed specifically for this borrower, this business, this purpose, and this moment in their financial life. That is the job. And when it is done well, the borrower knows it.

A Structure Checklist Before the Credit Memo

Before any commercial loan structure is finalized, a disciplined lender confirms: Does the loan type match the purpose? Is the term appropriate for the useful life of the asset? Does the amortization align with expected cash flow? Is the loan-to-value consistent with realistic liquidation value? Are financial covenants set at levels that provide meaningful early warning? Is the guarantee structure appropriate for the ownership and risk profile? And does the full structure, taken together, tell the same story as the credit analysis that preceded it?

If every question can be answered confidently, the structure is ready. If any produces hesitation, the structure needs more work before it moves forward.

> *Practitioner's Note: New commercial bankers often underestimate the significance of structure because structural decisions are made after the credit analysis, and the credit analysis feels like the hard part. It isn't. A perfectly underwritten credit with the wrong structure will perform worse than a modestly underwritten credit with the right one. Structure is where your understanding of the business, the cash flow, and the risk is translated into contractual reality. Get the analysis right. Then get the structure right. In that order.*

CHAPTER 10

From Conversation to Credit: The Lender's Mindset

There is a difference between a banker who does commercial lending and a commercial banker.

It is not a difference of title or tenure. It is not determined by how many loans are on the books or how many years have been spent in the industry. It is a difference of mindset, a fundamental orientation toward the work that shapes every conversation, every file, every credit decision, and every relationship a banker builds over the course of a career.

This book has been building toward that mindset. Not by defining it abstractly, but by assembling its components one chapter at a time, the shift from products to custom built, the discipline of Story Before Structure, the 5 Cs and a G, the literacy to read a financial statement as a narrative rather than a scorecard, the structural judgment to match a loan to its purpose, and the integrity to present the full picture rather than the favorable one.

This final chapter is about how those components come together, not as a checklist to be completed before a credit memo is written, but as a way of thinking that operates continuously, across every interaction, from the first conversation to the last payment on the last loan in a decades-long relationship.

The Mindset Starts in the Conversation

Commercial banking relationships rarely announce themselves as such. They begin in ordinary moments, a referral from a branch manager, a conversation at a business event, a call from someone who heard your name from someone else. They begin in deposit conversations, cash management meetings, and introductory lunches where no specific financial need has yet been identified.

The commercial banker who is waiting for a loan request before they engage is not building relationships. They are waiting for transactions. The lender's mindset is active before the loan request exists. It is present in the deposit conversation, listening for what the business does, how it operates, where it is trying to go, and what it needs from a banking partner.

A commercial banker who listens well in a deposit conversation will know more about a borrower before the formal loan request arrives than most bankers learn during the underwriting process. They will have context, history, and the beginning of a judgment about character and management competence, all of it arrived naturally through genuine engagement.

The Mindset in the Loan Request

When the loan request arrives, the lender's mindset organizes it immediately around the story. Not the amount. Not the purpose. Not the financial package. The story.

Who is this borrower, and what do I already know about them? What does this business do, and how does it make money? Why is this request being made now? What is the borrower trying to accomplish? Why does this relationship belong on our books?

The lender's mindset does not wait for the financial statements to form a preliminary view. It forms that view from the conversation, from the story the borrower tells, the way they tell it, the questions they can answer readily and the ones they deflect. Then the financial statements arrive. And the lender's mindset approaches them as a test of the story. Does the income statement support the narrative? Does the balance sheet reflect the position described? Does the cash flow tell the same story as the DSCR estimated from the conversation?

The Mindset in the Analysis

Credit analysis is not arithmetic. It is judgment supported by arithmetic.

A DSCR of 1.30 tells you the business generates thirty percent more cash flow than its debt service requires. But a lender's mindset asks: what does that DSCR look like in a stress scenario? What if the largest customer does not renew? What if material costs increase by fifteen percent? The ratio says 1.30. The lender's mindset asks whether 1.30 is enough given the specific vulnerabilities of this business.

The lender's mindset is not skeptical for the sake of skepticism. It is rigorous for the sake of accuracy. It asks the questions that the numbers alone cannot answer, and it holds itself to the same standard it applies to the borrower's narrative. No convenient assumptions. No figures accepted without understanding what produced them.

The Mindset in the Decision

Commercial credit decisions are not binary. They are a considered judgment about the nature of the relationship, the quality of the credit, the appropriateness of the structure, and the institution's appetite for the specific combination of risk and reward the deal represents.

It is not a sales decision. The institution's revenue goals and the lender's production targets are not credit considerations. A lender who allows production pressure to influence credit judgment is doing sales with a credit memo attached.

It is not a relationship preservation decision. The desire to maintain a positive relationship with a valued borrower is not a credit consideration. Good relationships survive credit declines when the decline is delivered with transparency, respect, and a genuine explanation of what would need to change.

The credit decision is a judgment call made by a person who has done the work, who has heard the story, tested it against the numbers, evaluated the risk through the 5 Cs and a G, structured the deal appropriately, and formed an honest view of whether this relationship makes sense. That judgment call is the job.

The Mindset After the Decision

The lender's mindset does not end at closing. Portfolio monitoring is not a compliance exercise. It is a continuation of the analytical work that began before the loan was made. When annual financial statements arrive, they are read, and the covenants are tested. When a borrower misses a payment, it is not informally waived. It is a signal that deserves a direct conversation.

Problems that are identified early can be managed. Problems that are identified late can only be survived. The lender who manages their portfolio with the same rigor they apply to underwriting will produce credits that perform well not just at origination but across the full arc of the relationship.

The Mindset as a Practice

Everything described in this chapter is a practice. Not a credential. Not a set of techniques mastered in a training program and then applied mechanically. A practice is something you do every day, in every relevant context, with deliberate attention to whether you are doing it well.

The practice of the lender's mindset includes a few commitments that experienced commercial bankers carry into every engagement.

Tell the story first. Before the numbers, before the structure, before the credit memo, tell the story. If you cannot tell it clearly, you do not understand the credit well enough to advance it. The clarity required to tell a story well is the same clarity required to make a sound credit decision.

Build custom. Every business is different. Every credit is different. Every structure should reflect the specific circumstances of the specific borrower rather than a template applied for convenience.

Understand what custom built actually means. The absence of standard products in commercial banking is not a limitation. It is the most powerful tool in the commercial banker's kit. If you can understand the need completely, quantify the risk honestly, and build a structure that is genuinely beneficial to both the borrower and the institution, you can build it. There is no shelf to limit the possible. There is only the discipline required to build what the risk actually supports. Commercial banking, done well, is a design discipline. The canvas is wide. The responsibility is to fill it with structures that work.

Apply the full framework. The 5 Cs and a G are not a menu from which a lender selects the most favorable indicators. They are a complete framework, and every element deserves genuine evaluation on every credit.

Hold the story to the same standard as the numbers. Inconsistencies between narrative and data are not minor discrepancies to be smoothed over. They are questions that require answers before the analysis moves forward.

Manage the portfolio as carefully as the pipeline. The credits already on the books deserve the same analytical attention as the ones being evaluated for approval.

Be the banker who shows up. Show up when there is no transaction pending. Call when the news from their industry is significant. Ask how the business is doing when there is no credit event requiring the question. Be the banker who knows the business well enough to add value outside the lending conversation.

What Comes Next

This book was designed to give you a foundation. The relationship foundation. The financial statement foundation. The 5 Cs and a G. The structural logic. The lender's mindset that holds all of it together.

What this book has not given you is the depth. The deep credit mechanics of specific loan types, the SBA loan, the construction loan, the commercial real estate acquisition, the C&I facility, the acquisition financing. The industry-specific risk frameworks. The advanced cash flow modeling. That depth lives in two places.

If you are heading into commercial lending, if the credit work, the financial analysis, and the deal structuring are where your professional path is taking you, your next book is ***Loan by Design***™. It picks up exactly where this one leaves off, taking the foundational framework established here and building the full structure of commercial credit practice on top of it.

If you are heading into the deposit and cash management side, if the relationship conversation, the operating cycle analysis, and the connection between how a business manages its cash and how a banking institution can add value are where your focus lies, your next book is ***The Cash Discipline*** ™. It takes the deposit foundation introduced in these pages and builds the full framework of business deposit strategy and cash management.

You may be heading to both. The commercial banker who understands lending and deposits, who can have the full relationship conversation with a business owner, is the commercial banker most valuable to their institution and most useful to the businesses they serve. That is the commercial banker this book was written to help you become.

A Final Word

There is a moment that happens to commercial bankers who have been at this long enough, who have seen enough deals, managed enough relationships, and made enough decisions across enough market cycles to have developed genuine pattern recognition.

The moment is this: a borrower walks in, and before the first financial statement has been reviewed, before the first ratio has been calculated, before the credit memo has been drafted, the experienced lender already has a sense of the deal. Not a conclusion. A sense. A preliminary orientation formed from the way the story was told, the questions the borrower could answer and the ones they couldn't, the consistency between the narrative and the lender's knowledge of the industry, and the feeling, built from years of practice, of whether this is the kind of relationship that belongs on their institution's books.

That sense is not infallible. It requires testing. It requires the discipline of the full analytical process applied rigorously to confirm or correct the preliminary judgment. But it exists. And it is the product of everything described in this book, applied repeatedly, reflected on honestly, and refined across years of practice.

You are at the beginning of building that sense. The foundation is laid. The framework is yours. The practice starts now.

Go learn the business. Go listen to the stories. Go build something custom.

And when you sit down across from a borrower for the first time and realize, not with panic, but with the quiet confidence of someone who has prepared, that you know what you're looking at:

That is the moment this book was written for.

> *Practitioner's Note: The lender's mindset is not a destination. It is a practice, built through every conversation, every file, every*

decision, and every relationship across a career. The measure of that practice is not how many loans you approved. It is how many you understood. The ones you declined well. The ones you structured right. The ones you monitored closely enough to catch a problem before it became a loss. Start there. Build from there. The rest of the work will teach you what no book can, and it will teach you faster than you expect, if you stay curious and stay honest. Go do the work.

APPENDIX A

The Story Workshop

Learning to Tell the Complete Story Before You Open the File

Why This Appendix Exists

Throughout*Banking the Business*, one discipline has been emphasized above all others: tell the story first. Before the financial statements. Before the ratios. Before the credit memo is drafted or the committee presentation is prepared, tell the story.

That discipline is easy to agree with in principle. It is harder to apply in practice, because most bankers have never been shown what a complete story actually looks like, or how far short of complete the stories they typically tell actually fall.

What follows is a single loan request, a medical practice seeking to acquire the commercial real estate it currently occupies, told three different ways. The first is what most bankers bring to the table. The second is better but still incomplete. The third is what an experienced commercial lender expects to hear before a file moves forward.

The Scenario

Borrower: Westside Family Medicine, LLC. Principal: Dr. Angela Reyes, sole owner and practicing physician. Request: $1,850,000 commercial real estate term loan to purchase the medical office building the practice currently leases. Property: 6,200 square foot single-tenant medical office building, owner-occupied. Current lease: Month-to-month, following expiration of a five-year lease term. Practice: Primary care, established 11 years, employing Dr. Reyes and two nurse practitioners.

Version One: The Weak Story

What most bankers say when they haven't done the work.

* * *

"Dr. Reyes has been a client of ours for about three years. She runs a family medicine practice out on the west side, been there for eleven years, good reputation in the community. She's looking to purchase the building she's currently leasing. The asking price is two point one million, she's putting down two hundred and fifty thousand, so the loan request is one point eight five million. The practice has been profitable, her personal credit is clean, and she wants to stop paying rent and start building equity. It seems like a pretty straightforward owner-occupied real estate deal. I'd like to get this in front of the committee."

* * *

What's Missing, and Why It Matters

This story is not wrong. Every sentence is accurate. But what's missing represents the majority of the actual credit risk in this transaction.

The practice's financial performance is described with one word: profitable. Profitable how much? How consistently? What does revenue look like over three years? What is the DSCR? A committee approving this based on "the practice has been profitable" is not doing credit analysis.

The revenue composition is completely absent. Medical practices have a payer mix, the percentage of revenue from private insurance, Medicare, Medicaid, and self-pay. Payer mix drives reimbursement rates, collection timelines, and revenue stability. None of that appears in this story.

Physician dependency has not been mentioned. Westside Family Medicine is a single-physician practice. Dr. Reyes is not just the owner, she is the practice. What happens if she becomes ill or unable to practice? What disability insurance exists?

The property is underexamined. What is the appraised value? The LTV? Is this a specialized medical build-out that would limit secondary market appeal?

The lease situation is a flag that hasn't been raised. Month-to-month after a five-year expiration is not a neutral fact. Why is the lease month-to-month? Was a renewal negotiated and failed?

The guarantor has been reduced to a credit score. "Her personal credit is clean" is not a guarantor assessment. What is Dr. Reyes's personal net worth? What liquid assets does she hold outside the business?

Version Two: The Partial Story

What a banker who has done some of the work says. Better, but still not complete.

* * *

"Dr. Angela Reyes is the sole owner and practicing physician at Westside Family Medicine, a primary care practice she founded eleven years ago. The practice currently occupies a 6,200 square foot medical office building under a month-to-month lease, and Dr. Reyes is requesting a loan of one point eight five million to purchase that building at an agreed price of two point one million. She's contributing two hundred and fifty thousand in equity at closing, approximately twelve percent down. The practice has been with us for three years. Revenue for the trailing twelve months was one point four million, up from one point two million two years ago. Net income after compensation to Dr. Reyes was approximately two hundred and twenty thousand dollars. We estimate the proposed debt service at approximately one hundred and thirty two thousand dollars annually, which produces a DSCR of roughly one point six times. Dr. Reyes's personal credit score is seven sixty two, and her personal financial statement reflects a net worth of approximately nine hundred thousand dollars. The property appraised at two point zero five million, putting our LTV at approximately ninety percent. I think this is a solid credit. I'd like to move it forward."

* * *

What's Better, and What's Still Missing

This version is meaningfully stronger. There is financial detail, a DSCR estimate, some guarantor information, and existing relationship context. But several critical gaps remain.

The payer mix is still absent. A committee member who understands medical practice lending will ask about payer mix immediately. The banker should have answered this question before it was asked.

Physician dependency has been identified but not addressed. Noting that Dr. Reyes is the sole physician is accurate. It is not sufficient. What disability coverage exists? Can the nurse practitioners maintain some revenue during an absence?

The LTV has a problem that hasn't been addressed. The property appraised at two point zero five million. Purchase price is two point one million. LTV based on appraised value is approximately ninety percent, above the typical threshold. How does the banker propose to address this?

The guarantor assessment is still shallow. Nine hundred thousand dollars in net worth sounds substantial. But its composition matters. If most of it is illiquid, equity in the practice and a personal residence, it is a very different guarantee than nine hundred thousand in liquid investment accounts.

Version Three: The Complete Story

What an experienced commercial banker presents. The story holds before the file opens.

* * *

"Let me tell you about Westside Family Medicine and why I think this is both a sound credit and a relationship our institution should want to own for a long time.

Dr. Angela Reyes founded Westside Family Medicine eleven years ago as a solo primary care practice. Today it operates from a 6,200 square foot medical office building on the west side, employs Dr. Reyes and two nurse practitioners, and serves an established patient panel of approximately 2,400 active patients. The practice has built a strong community reputation, Dr. Reyes has been named to the regional preferred provider network for two of the three major commercial carriers in our market.

The request is a one point eight five million dollar commercial real estate term loan. I want to address the appraisal gap upfront, the property appraised at two point zero five million, putting our LTV at approximately ninety percent. I have discussed this with Dr. Reyes and she has agreed to bring additional equity to closing to bring the LTV to eighty percent, either through an increased cash contribution or by pledging her investment account, approximately three hundred and forty thousand in liquid securities, as additional collateral.

Revenue for the trailing twelve months was one point four million, up from one point two million two years ago. Revenue composition is approximately forty-eight percent commercial insurance, thirty-one percent Medicare, fourteen percent Medicaid, and seven percent self-pay and other. Collections are running at approximately ninety-four percent of billed charges, strong for this practice type.

Net income after Dr. Reyes's physician compensation of three hundred thousand dollars was two hundred and twenty thousand. We have analyzed cash flow on a three-year average. Proposed annual debt service is one hundred and thirty two thousand dollars. Global DSCR including Dr. Reyes's personal obligations is one point four eight times on the three-year average, above our minimum and above our preferred threshold even under a ten percent revenue stress scenario.

I want to be direct about the concentration risk: Dr. Reyes is the sole physician. I have reviewed her disability insurance coverage: she carries an own-occupation disability policy with a benefit of twenty thousand dollars per month, activated after a ninety-day elimination period. The two nurse practitioners are credentialed independently and capable of maintaining approximately forty percent of practice revenue during a physician absence of up to six months. This concentration risk is real. The mitigation is the quality of the guarantor, the strength of the collateral, and the structure of the loan.

The guarantor picture is strong. Dr. Reyes's personal net worth is nine hundred and ten thousand dollars. Approximately three hundred and forty thousand, thirty-seven percent, is in liquid investment accounts independent of the practice and the real estate. She is not overleveraged personally and has meaningful liquidity outside the assets being financed.

The month-to-month lease requires explanation. The original five-year lease expired fourteen months ago. Dr. Reyes attempted to negotiate a renewal but the landlord was unwilling to commit to a long-term lease because he was already exploring a sale. The month-to-month arrangement was mutually agreed as a bridge to a sale process that has now arrived. The practice has right of first refusal, which is how this purchase opportunity arose.

Now, why does this institution want this relationship? Westside Family Medicine has banked with us for three years. Their operating accounts carry an average daily balance of approximately forty thousand dollars. If we close this transaction, this becomes a full commercial relationship. Dr. Reyes is forty-one years old, at the beginning of a career with significant wealth accumulation ahead. The personal banking, investment, and financial planning relationship that comes with a physician at this stage of practice growth is exactly the profile our institution has identified as a strategic priority.

This is a sound commercial credit with one clearly identified and clearly mitigated concentration risk. The cash flow supports the debt service with adequate margin, the guarantor is financially strong and independent of the collateral, and the collateral structure, with the additional equity contribution, is appropriate for the asset type. I am recommending approval."

* * *

What Makes This Story Complete

The third version does several things the first two do not.

It leads with context, not with the request. It identifies the primary risk and addresses it directly, naming physician dependency, quantifying the mitigation, and being honest about its limits. It answers the payer mix question before it is asked. It resolves the appraisal gap before the committee has to raise it. It characterizes the guarantor's net worth by composition, not just by size. It explains the month-to-month lease. And it makes the strategic case for the institution, not just for the borrower.

That is the complete story. And when it holds together before the file is opened, everything that follows is confirmation rather than discovery.

The Story Template

Use this framework as a self-check before you present any commercial loan request. If you cannot answer every question, you are not ready to tell the story. This template is the self-check version of the Story Test introduced in Chapter 8. Use both.

The Borrower: Who are they, the people behind the business? How long have they been in this industry? What do you know about their character and track record?

The Business: What does it do, and how does it actually make money? What is the revenue model, the customer base, and the operating cycle? What makes this business competitively positioned, or vulnerable?

The Numbers: What does the financial performance look like over three years? What is the revenue composition and quality? What is the DSCR, and does it hold under a stress scenario?

The Request: What are they asking for, in specific terms? Why now? Does the structure fit the purpose? Are there any structural issues requiring resolution before the deal moves forward?

The Primary Risk: What is the single biggest risk in this credit? Have you named it directly? Have you described the mitigation honestly?

The Collateral and Guarantor: What is the secondary repayment picture, specifically? What is the collateral worth in a realistic liquidation scenario? What does the guarantor actually bring, its composition, liquidity, and independence from the assets being financed?

The Relationship: Why does this institution want this credit? What is the full banking relationship? What does this borrower represent over a five- to ten-year horizon?

The Story Test: Can you tell all of the above, out loud, to someone who has not seen the file, in a way that is clear, consistent, and internally logical, and have the story hold together under questions?

The story is not a formality. It is the proof that you understand the deal. Everything else, the financial analysis, the structure, the credit memo, is evidence in support of a judgment you have already formed. Form the judgment first. Then build the case.

APPENDIX B

The Commercial Banking Glossary

The Language of Commercial Lending, Defined the Way Practitioners Use It

A Note on This Glossary

Every profession has a language. Commercial banking has one of the denser ones. When a retail banker walks into their first credit committee, they often encounter that language without a translation guide. Terms are used with the assumption that everyone in the room already knows them.

This glossary exists to close that gap. Every term is defined the way a senior commercial lender would define it to a new hire, plainly, practically, and with enough context to understand not just what the term means but why it matters. Read it once straight through before your first credit committee. Then keep it nearby.

Accounts Payable (AP)

Money a business owes to its suppliers for goods or services it has received but not yet paid for. AP is a current liability on the balance sheet. A business that is stretching its payables, paying suppliers more slowly than normal, may be managing a cash flow problem not yet visible in the income statement. *See also: Working Capital, Current Liabilities.*

Accounts Receivable (AR)

Money owed to a business by its customers for goods delivered or services rendered but not yet collected. The quality of receivables, how old they are, how concentrated, and how reliably collected, matters as much as the dollar amount. *See also: Aging Schedule, Borrowing Base, Concentration Risk.*

Advance Rate

The percentage of a collateral asset's value that a lender will advance against. Advance rates reflect a lender's judgment about realistic liquidation value, the cushion between the loan amount and what the collateral would actually yield in a distressed sale. *See also: Loan-to-Value Ratio, Collateral.*

Aging Schedule

A breakdown of accounts receivable organized by how long each invoice has been outstanding, typically in thirty, sixty, ninety, and over-ninety-day buckets. The aging schedule reveals the quality of receivables that the balance sheet total obscures. *See also: Accounts Receivable.*

Amortization

The process of repaying a loan's principal balance over time through scheduled payments. A fully amortizing loan reaches zero balance at maturity. A partially amortizing loan leaves a balloon payment due at maturity. *See also: Balloon Payment, Term Loan.*

Annual Cleanup (aka Resting Period)

A requirement that a revolving line of credit be paid to a zero balance for a specified period, typically thirty consecutive days, at least once per year. The annual cleanup, or resting period, confirms that the line is functioning as working capital financing rather than permanent capital. A line that cannot achieve annual cleanup indicates the borrower may be structurally dependent on borrowed funds to operate. *See also: Line of Credit, Evergreen Line.*

Appraisal

A formal, independent estimate of the market value of a property or asset, conducted by a licensed appraiser. Lenders rely on appraisals to establish loan-to-value ratios and collateral positions. *See also: Loan-to-Value Ratio, Fair Market Value.*

Asset-Based Lending (ABL)

A lending structure in which the available amount under a credit facility is tied directly to the value of specific current assets, typically accounts receivable and inventory, rather than a fixed loan amount. *See also: Borrowing Base, Revolving Line of Credit.*

B

Balance Sheet

One of the three primary financial statements. The balance sheet is a snapshot of a business's financial position at a specific point in time. The fundamental equation: Assets = Liabilities + Equity. Commercial lenders read the balance sheet as a risk map, evaluating the relationships between assets, liabilities, and equity. *See also: Assets, Liabilities, Equity, Leverage.*

Balloon Payment

A large lump-sum payment due at the maturity of a loan that has been amortizing on a longer schedule than its term. Balloon payments create refinancing events that carry market and credit risk. *See also: Amortization, Maturity.*

Borrowing Base

In an asset-based lending structure, the calculation that determines how much a borrower can draw under their credit facility at any given time, typically a specified advance rate applied to eligible receivables plus a specified advance rate applied to eligible inventory. *See also: Asset-Based Lending, Advance Rate.*

Bridge Loan

A short-term loan designed to bridge a gap between two longer-term financing events. Bridge loans typically carry higher rates and shorter terms than permanent financing, and carry refinancing risk if anticipated permanent financing is delayed.

C

Capital Expenditure (CapEx)

Cash spent by a business to acquire, maintain, or improve its long-term physical assets. CapEx does not flow through the income statement as an expense, it is recorded as a balance sheet asset and depreciated over time. This is why EBITDA can overstate available cash flow for capital-intensive businesses. *See also: Depreciation, EBITDA, Free Cash Flow.*

Cash Flow Statement

One of the three primary financial statements. It reconciles net income to the actual cash generated and consumed by the business during the period. Organized into three sections: operating activities, investing activities, and financing activities. For commercial lenders, the operating section is most important. *See also: Operating Cash Flow, Free Cash Flow.*

Collateral

Assets pledged by a borrower to secure a loan, the secondary repayment source available to the lender if the primary repayment source fails. Collateral is a backstop, not a substitute for cash flow analysis. *See also: Primary Repayment Source, Secondary Repayment Source, UCC-1 Financing Statement.*

Commercial Real Estate (CRE)

Real property used for business purposes, office buildings, retail centers, industrial facilities, multifamily properties, hotels. Owner-occupied CRE, where the borrower's own business is the primary tenant, is evaluated differently than investor CRE, where collateral value depends on third-party tenant income. *See also: Loan-to-Value Ratio, Net Operating Income.*

Concentration Risk

The degree to which a business's revenue, receivables, or relationships depend on a small number of customers, industries, or geographies. Concentration risk is one of the most commonly underanalyzed risks in commercial lending. *See also: Accounts Receivable, Conditions.*

Covenant

A contractual obligation included in a loan agreement that the borrower must comply with over the life of the loan. Affirmative covenants require specific actions. Negative covenants prohibit specific actions without lender consent. Financial covenants establish minimum performance standards, typically minimum DSCR and maximum leverage ratios. Covenants are monitoring tools, not penalties. *See also: Debt Service Coverage Ratio, Technical Default.*

Current Assets

Assets expected to be converted to cash, sold, or consumed within the next twelve months, cash, accounts receivable, inventory, and prepaid expenses. *See also: Working Capital, Current Ratio.*

Current Liabilities

Obligations due within the next twelve months, accounts payable, accrued expenses, short-term debt, and the current portion of long-term debt. *See also: Working Capital, Current Ratio.*

Current Ratio

Current assets divided by current liabilities. A ratio below 1.0 means current liabilities exceed current assets, the business may struggle to meet near-term obligations. *See also: Working Capital.*

D

Debt Service

The total cash required to cover all principal and interest payments on outstanding loans over a given period, typically calculated annually. Includes all existing obligations plus the proposed new loan. *See also: Debt Service Coverage Ratio.*

Debt Service Coverage Ratio (DSCR)

Net operating income or free cash flow divided by total annual debt service. The single most important metric in commercial lending, it measures how many times over the business can cover its debt obligations from operating cash flow. A DSCR at or below 1.00 means the business cannot cover its debt from operations. Most lenders require a minimum of 1.20 to 1.25. *See also: Net Operating Income, Debt Service, Free Cash Flow.*

Deed of Trust

A legal instrument that transfers the title of a property to a trustee as security for a loan. Recording the deed of trust with the county establishes the lender's lien position on real property collateral. *See also: Collateral, Lien, Mortgage.*

Default

A borrower's failure to comply with the terms of a loan agreement. Payment default is the failure to make a scheduled payment. Technical default, the failure to comply with a covenant, gives the lender legal standing to act before the situation reaches payment default. *See also: Covenant, Technical Default.*

Depreciation

The accounting recognition that physical assets lose value over time. Depreciation is a non-cash expense, it reduces reported net income without consuming actual cash. Added back in EBITDA calculations. *See also: EBITDA, Capital Expenditure, Non-Cash Expense.*

Draw

A disbursement of funds under a credit facility, specifically under a construction loan or revolving line of credit. *See also: Construction Loan, Line of Credit.*

EBITDA

Earnings Before Interest, Taxes, Depreciation, and Amortization. An analytical measure used to evaluate operating performance independent of capital structure, tax situation, and non-cash adjustments. EBITDA is a starting point, not an ending point, it overstates available cash flow for capital-intensive businesses. *See also: Depreciation, Capital Expenditure, Free Cash Flow.*

Equity

The residual interest in a business's assets after all liabilities have been subtracted. In a real estate context, equity is the difference between property value and outstanding loan balance. Equity is the cushion that absorbs financial stress before creditors are affected. *See also: Leverage, Retained Earnings.*

Evergreen Line

A revolving line of credit that never returns to a zero balance, a structural warning sign indicating the borrower is using a working capital facility as permanent capital. Requires closer analysis of the business's underlying cash flow. *See also: Annual Cleanup, Line of Credit.*

F

Fair Market Value

The price at which an asset would change hands between a willing buyer and a willing seller, neither under compulsion. Generally higher than orderly liquidation value and significantly higher than forced liquidation value, which is why lenders apply advance rates rather than lending at full appraised value. *See also: Orderly Liquidation Value, Forced Liquidation Value.*

Forced Liquidation Value

The estimated proceeds achievable in a rapid, time-pressured sale. Can be dramatically lower than fair market value, particularly for specialized assets. *See also: Fair Market Value, Orderly Liquidation Value.*

Free Cash Flow

Operating cash flow minus capital expenditures required to maintain the business's productive capacity. The most honest measure of debt service capacity because it accounts for the actual cash demands of maintaining the business before any debt payments. *See also: EBITDA, Capital Expenditure, Operating Cash Flow.*

G

Global Cash Flow

A cash flow analysis combining the business's cash flow with the personal cash flow of the guarantor, presenting the complete picture of all resources available to service the proposed debt. *See also: Guarantor, Debt Service Coverage Ratio.*

Goodwill

The premium paid above the fair value of identifiable assets when one business acquires another. Goodwill has no independent liquidation value, cannot be sold separately, and is excluded from tangible net worth calculations. *See also: Intangible Assets, Tangible Net Worth.*

Gross Margin

Gross profit divided by revenue. Measures how much revenue the business retains after covering direct production costs. Declining gross margin, compression year over year, is a warning sign worth investigating directly. *See also: Gross Profit, Operating Margin.*

Gross Profit

Revenue minus cost of goods sold, what the business retains after covering the direct costs of producing its product or service. *See also: Gross Margin, Cost of Goods Sold.*

Guarantor

An individual or entity that agrees to be personally responsible for a loan obligation if the primary borrower fails to repay. The guarantor is the G in the 5 Cs and a G. Evaluating the guarantor, financial strength, liquidity, independence of assets, and character, is as important as evaluating the business itself. *See also: Personal Guarantee, Global Cash Flow.*

I

Intangible Assets

Assets that lack physical substance but have economic value, patents, trademarks, customer lists, non-compete agreements, and goodwill. Treated conservatively in credit analysis. Goodwill is excluded from tangible net worth calculations. *See also: Goodwill, Tangible Net Worth.*

L

Leverage

The degree to which a business has used debt to finance its assets. Leverage amplifies both returns and risk. Thin equity relative to debt means less cushion to absorb stress before creditors are affected. *See also: Debt-to-Equity Ratio, Equity.*

Lien

A legal claim against an asset that secures a debt obligation. A first lien gives the lender first priority in recovering from collateral. A second lien is subordinate. Lien position matters enormously in a default scenario. *See also: UCC-1 Financing Statement, Deed of Trust, Priority.*

Line of Credit

A revolving credit facility that allows a borrower to draw funds up to a specified maximum, repay, and draw again, on an as-needed basis. Designed for working capital, cyclical, self-liquidating operating needs. *See also: Revolving Credit, Annual Cleanup, Evergreen Line.*

Loan-to-Value Ratio (LTV)

The ratio of the loan amount to the appraised value of the collateral. Measures the cushion between the outstanding loan balance and the collateral value. As LTV increases, the cushion decreases. *See also: Advance Rate, Appraisal, Collateral.*

M

Maturity

The date on which the final payment on a loan is due and the outstanding balance must be repaid in full. For balloon loans, the maturity date creates a refinancing event that carries market and credit risk. *See also: Balloon Payment, Amortization.*

Mortgage

A legal instrument that gives a lender a security interest in real property as collateral for a loan. Recording the mortgage establishes the lender's lien position against the property. *See also: Deed of Trust, Lien, Collateral.*

Net Operating Income (NOI)

Gross revenue minus operating expenses, before debt service. The numerator in the DSCR calculation, the cash available to service debt. The most direct measure of debt service capacity. *See also: Debt Service Coverage Ratio, Operating Expenses.*

Non-Cash Expense

An expense that reduces reported net income without consuming actual cash. Depreciation and amortization are the most common non-cash expenses. Added back in cash flow analysis to produce a truer picture of actual cash generation. *See also: Depreciation, EBITDA, Cash Flow Statement.*

O

Operating Cash Flow

The cash a business generates from its core operations during a period, as reported on the cash flow statement. Starts with net income and adjusts for non-cash expenses and working capital changes. The primary measure of repayment capacity in commercial credit analysis. *See also: Free Cash Flow, Cash Flow Statement, DSCR.*

Operating Margin

Operating income divided by revenue. Measures how efficiently the business converts revenue into profit after both direct costs and overhead. Declining operating margin indicates cost pressure, pricing weakness, or both. *See also: EBITDA, Gross Margin.*

Orderly Liquidation Value

The estimated proceeds achievable in a liquidation conducted over a reasonable period of time. Lower than fair market value. The benchmark most commercial lenders use for equipment and inventory collateral. *See also: Fair Market Value, Forced Liquidation Value.*

P

Payer Mix

In healthcare and medical practice lending, the composition of a practice's revenue by reimbursement source, commercial insurance, Medicare, Medicaid, and self-pay. Payer mix determines reimbursement rates, collection timelines, and revenue stability. A primary credit consideration in medical practice lending. *See also: Concentration Risk, Revenue.*

Personal Financial Statement

A document summarizing an individual's personal assets, liabilities, and net worth, the personal equivalent of a business balance sheet. Required from guarantors to evaluate the quality and independence of the personal guarantee. *See also: Guarantor, Global Cash Flow.*

Personal Guarantee

A legal commitment by an individual to be personally responsible for a loan obligation if the primary borrower fails to repay. An unlimited guarantee obligates the guarantor for the full outstanding balance. A limited guarantee caps the obligation at a specified amount. The guarantee is only as strong as the financial substance behind it. *See also: Guarantor, Personal Financial Statement.*

Primary Repayment Source

The first and preferred source of loan repayment, operating cash flow generated by the business from its normal operations. Collateral and guarantees are secondary, they exist in case the primary source fails, not as justification for making the loan when the primary source isn't there. *See also: Secondary Repayment Source, Collateral, DSCR.*

Retained Earnings

The cumulative net income a business has generated over its history, minus any distributions paid to owners. Positive retained earnings indicate a history of profitable operation. Negative retained earnings indicate the business has lost more than it has earned, or distributed more than it has generated. *See also: Equity, Distributions.*

Revolving Credit

A credit facility that allows a borrower to draw, repay, and draw again, up to a specified maximum, on a flexible, as-needed basis. Appropriate for cyclical working capital needs. A healthy revolving facility cycles, it goes up when the business needs cash and comes back down when collections arrive. *See also: Line of Credit, Annual Cleanup, Evergreen Line.*

S

Secondary Repayment Source

The fallback repayment mechanism available to a lender if the primary repayment source fails. Typically consists of collateral liquidation and the personal guarantee. Protects the institution in a default scenario, but does not substitute for a credible primary repayment source. *See also: Primary Repayment Source, Collateral, Guarantor.*

Stress Test

An analytical exercise that evaluates how a borrower's DSCR holds up under adverse conditions, typically a ten or fifteen percent revenue decline, a significant cost increase, or an interest rate increase. A credit whose DSCR collapses under moderate stress is more fragile than one whose coverage remains adequate. *See also: DSCR, Sensitivity Analysis.*

T

Tangible Net Worth

Total equity minus intangible assets. Strips out goodwill and other intangibles to produce a more conservative measure of actual net worth available to absorb losses. *See also: Goodwill, Intangible Assets, Equity.*

Technical Default

A covenant violation that gives the lender legal standing to declare the loan in default, even in the absence of a missed payment. Technical defaults are early warning mechanisms, they enable the institution to act constructively before the situation deteriorates to payment default. *See also: Covenant, Default.*

Term Loan

A fixed advance of capital repaid over a defined period through scheduled payments of principal and interest. Used to finance one-time capital needs, equipment purchases, real estate acquisitions, business expansions. Unlike a revolving line of credit, a term loan cannot be re-drawn after principal is repaid. *See also: Amortization, Revolving Credit.*

UCC-1 Financing Statement

A public notice document filed with the appropriate state authority to establish a lender's security interest in personal property collateral. Filing a UCC-1 perfects the lender's security interest, establishing its legal priority claim against the collateral relative to other creditors. *See also: Lien, Collateral, Priority.*

Working Capital

Current assets minus current liabilities. Measures the liquidity available to fund a business's day-to-day operations. Positive working capital indicates a business can meet its near-term obligations from existing liquid resources. *See also: Current Assets, Current Liabilities, Current Ratio.*

*This glossary covers the core vocabulary of commercial banking at the level required to engage productively in credit conversations, read a credit memo, and follow a loan committee discussion. The terms not found here will be found in*Loan by Design™ *and* The Cash Discipline, *where the deeper discipline of each subject is developed fully.*

APPENDIX C

The 10 Things Retail Bankers Get Wrong About Commercial Lending

The Most Common Mistakes in the Transition, and How to Correct Them

A Note on This List

This is not a list of technical errors. Retail bankers transitioning into commercial lending are generally smart, capable, and motivated. They don't fail because they can't learn the mechanics. They struggle because they carry mental models from retail banking that were entirely correct in their original context, and are quietly wrong in the new one.

The ten mistakes that follow are orientation mistakes. Read this list before your first commercial credit conversation. Read it again after your first six months. The items that feel most uncomfortable the second time are the ones still doing the most damage.

1. Leading With the Product Instead of the Problem

The mistake: A retail banker's instinct, when sitting across from a business owner, is to reach for a solution. The borrower mentions cash flow, the banker's mind goes immediately to a line of credit. The solution arrives before the problem is fully understood.

Why it happens: Retail banking rewards product knowledge and fast matching. That speed is a virtue in a consumer context.

Why it's wrong in commercial banking: Business needs are rarely as simple as they appear in the first conversation. A business owner who says they need a line of credit because cash flow is tight may have a short-term liquidity need that a line will solve, or they may have a structural cash flow problem that a line will temporarily mask.

The correction: Lead with questions, not products. Before any solution is suggested, make sure you can answer: what is this business actually trying to accomplish, and what is the real source of the need? The right structure follows from a complete understanding of the problem.

2. Treating the Credit Score as the Credit Decision

The mistake: When retail bankers move into commercial lending, many continue to reach for the credit score first, and to treat a strong personal credit score as the primary indicator of creditworthiness.

Why it happens: The credit score reflex is deeply ingrained by years of consumer underwriting. It produced good decisions in the retail context.

Why it's wrong in commercial banking: A business owner with a 750 credit score can run a business that generates insufficient cash flow to service its debt. The credit score reflects personal repayment behavior, not the operating performance of the business.

The correction: Pull the credit report, it matters. But pull it after you've formed a preliminary view of the business's cash flow story. The credit score should inform your character and guarantor analysis. Cash flow drives the capacity decision.

3. Confusing Profit With Cash Flow

The mistake: When a borrower says the business is profitable, the retail banker hears: the business can repay the loan.

Why it happens: In personal finance, income and cash are largely the same concept. That equivalence does not hold for businesses.

Why it's wrong in commercial banking: A business can be profitable and cash flow negative simultaneously. Revenue recognized but not collected, inventory purchased but not sold, equipment bought and capitalized, principal payments not flowing through the income statement, all of these create gaps between reported profit and available cash.

The correction: Never accept "the business is profitable" as a cash flow assessment. Ask specifically about operating cash flow, free cash flow, and DSCR. Profit is reported. Cash flow is real. Only one of them repays a loan.

4. Over-Relying on Collateral

The mistake: When the cash flow analysis is thin or the story doesn't hold together, the retail banker reaches for collateral.

Why it happens: Collateral is tangible. It can be valued, documented, and pointed to. In consumer lending, collateral is often the primary underwriting basis.

Why it's wrong in commercial banking: Collateral is the second way out. A loan approved primarily because the collateral looks good, where the cash flow analysis is weak, is a liquidation plan with a loan attached. Liquidation plans rarely execute as cleanly as the original analysis suggested.

The correction: Underwrite the loan as though the collateral doesn't exist. Build the credit case on cash flow, capacity, and the full 5 Cs and a G. Then confirm the collateral is there, properly valued and properly secured, as the secondary protection.

5. Thinking in Products Instead of Custom-Built Solutions

The mistake: The retail banker approaches a business banking relationship looking for the right product to match to the customer's need.

Why it happens: Retail banking is built around products. That framework produces good retail bankers.

Why it's wrong in commercial banking: No two businesses are the same. The line of credit that works for a staffing company is structured differently than the one that works for a seasonal retailer. In commercial banking, you build around the business, and if you can quantify the risk and the structure is mutually beneficial, you can build it.

The correction: Replace "which product fits this borrower?" with "what does this business actually need, and can we build that?" The answer may look like a standard instrument. But it should always result from genuine inquiry into the business, not a reflexive product match.

6. Waiting for the Loan Request to Start Building the Relationship

The mistake: The retail banker waits. A business owner opens a checking account, the banker processes it. The business owner eventually comes in with a loan request, and now the banker pays attention.

Why it happens: Retail banking is largely transactional. The relationship exists within the transaction.

Why it's wrong in commercial banking: The deposit relationship is the beginning of the credit relationship. The average daily balances tell you about cash flow cycle. The payroll patterns tell you about the workforce. The merchant deposits tell you about revenue timing. Every interaction before the loan request is an opportunity to build the understanding that makes the credit relationship work.

The correction: Treat every business banking interaction as the first chapter of a longer story. Ask questions. Show genuine interest in where the business is going. Be present between transactions. The banker who knows the business before the loan request arrives will be a better lender and a more trusted partner.

7. Presenting the Numbers Before the Story

The mistake: The new commercial banker opens the credit memo, runs the ratios, calculates the DSCR, and brings the numbers to the senior lender as the basis for the recommendation.

Why it happens: Numbers feel like the objective part of commercial lending. Leading with numbers feels rigorous.

Why it's wrong in commercial banking: Numbers without context are data, not analysis. A DSCR of 1.35 for a single-physician practice whose sole owner is 62 years old is a different credit than a DSCR of 1.35 for a diversified manufacturing company with strong management depth. The numbers are the same. The story is entirely different.

The correction: Story Before Structure, every time, without exception. Before the financial analysis is presented, the story must be told. The numbers test the story. They do not replace it.

8. Treating the Annual Review as a Formality

The mistake: The loan closes. A year later, annual financial statements arrive. The banker files them, notes the loan is still current, and moves on.

Why it happens: Portfolio monitoring feels administrative compared to origination. In institutions where production is the primary metric, time spent monitoring existing credits is time not spent building new ones.

Why it's wrong in commercial banking: The annual review is a continuation of the credit analysis that justified the original approval. A business whose revenue is declining year over year is sending a signal. A covenant being approached but not yet breached is sending a signal. Problems identified early can be managed. Problems identified at default can only be survived.

The correction: Treat every annual review with the same rigor as the original underwriting. Test the covenants. Update the DSCR. Read the financial statements, don't just file them. And call the borrower proactively. That call is one of the most relationship-building acts a commercial banker can perform.

9. Underestimating the Guarantor

The mistake: The personal guarantee is collected, filed, and referenced in the credit memo as a credit enhancement. The guarantor's personal financial statement is reviewed at a summary level, net worth noted, credit pulled, box checked.

Why it happens: In consumer lending, the personal guarantee doesn't exist in the same form. The concept is new to retail bankers and is often introduced as a procedural requirement rather than a credit consideration.

Why it's wrong in commercial banking: The guarantor is the G in the 5 Cs and a G, and the guarantee is only as strong as the financial substance behind it. A guarantee backed by a guarantor whose net worth is concentrated in the business being financed provides very limited independent protection.

The correction: Evaluate the guarantor with the same rigor you apply to the business. What is their net worth, and what is its composition? How much is liquid and independent of the business being financed? What personal obligations do they carry? The guarantee is a credit decision in its own right.

10. Approving the Deal Instead of Making the Right Decision

The mistake: A deal arrives that is close, not quite strong enough on cash flow, a little thin on collateral, a story that mostly holds together. The banker approves it. The approval felt like a win. Eighteen months later, it doesn't.

Why it happens: Retail banking conditions bankers to treat approval as the successful outcome. That orientation is deeply ingrained and reinforced by production metrics.

Why it's wrong in commercial banking: The goal in commercial lending is not the approval. It is the right decision. The only failure in commercial credit is making the wrong decision, and the wrong decision is almost always an approval that shouldn't have been one.

The correction: Redefine what a win looks like. A win is a credit decision that holds up, made with complete information, honest analysis, and genuine judgment. A declined credit that was correctly declined is a win. Trust that the right decisions, made consistently, produce the kind of portfolio that reflects well on the banker who built it.

A Final Word on This List

Every item on this list is a mistake made by good bankers who were trained well for a different job. The retail banking foundation you bring into commercial lending is real and valuable. What this list asks of you is something specific: the willingness to recognize where your existing mental models need to be rebuilt, and to do that rebuilding deliberately, honestly, and before the mistakes on this list become entries in your own experience.

The commercial banking mindset is not born. It is built, through every conversation, every credit, every correction, and every year of deliberate practice in the discipline this book has introduced.

This list is part of the blueprint. What you build on it is up to you.

*The blueprint continues in*Loan by Design™, *for the credit path, and*The Cash Discipline, *for the deposit path. Choose your direction. Or take both.*

APPENDIX D

The Business Banking Conversation Guide

From the First Hello to the First Credit Conversation

How to Use This Guide

Business banking conversations don't follow scripts. Every business owner is different. Every relationship develops at its own pace. What this guide provides is a framework, a map of the conversation stages that typically mark the development of a business banking relationship, along with the questions that belong at each stage.

The stages are not always sequential. A borrower who arrives with a fully formed loan request has moved past stages one and two before the banker has had a chance to engage with them naturally. A long-standing deposit relationship may stay in stage two or three for years before a credit need emerges. Read each stage for its purpose, and use the questions when the conversation is ready for them.

One principle applies across all five stages: listen more than you talk. The questions are the work. The answers are the information. A banker who is formulating their next pitch while the borrower is answering the last question is not having a business banking conversation. They are waiting for their turn.

Cash Management and Deposit Definitions

The following terms appear throughout this guide and in business banking conversations generally. Understanding them, not just their definitions but their practical significance to a business owner, is the foundation of the Stage Two and Stage Three conversations.

Core Deposit and Cash Management Products

Business Checking Account: The primary operating account for a business. All day-to-day transactions flow through it, payroll, vendor payments, customer receipts, tax deposits. The operating account is the central node of the business banking relationship. A lender who monitors the operating account activity develops a real-time understanding of the business's cash flow cycle that no financial statement can replicate.

Business Savings / Money Market Account: Interest-bearing accounts for operating reserves, cash the business needs accessible but not immediately. Usually used for tax reserves, emergency operating funds, or short-term capital accumulation.

Analyzed Business Checking: A checking account structure designed for businesses with high transaction volumes. Monthly fees are offset against earnings credits based on the average collected balance. Common in treasury management relationships with larger businesses.

ACH (Automated Clearing House): The electronic payment network that processes most business transactions behind the scenes. ACH is used for direct deposit payroll, vendor payments, customer billing collections, and tax payments. Two directions: ACH credit (sending money out) and ACH debit (pulling money in, such as recurring customer billing). Businesses with significant vendor or payroll obligations process large ACH volumes; this makes ACH capabilities a meaningful point of differentiation in treasury management.

Wire Transfer: Same-day, irrevocable electronic funds transfers. Used for time-sensitive, high-dollar transactions, real estate closings, large vendor payments, international settlements. More expensive than ACH. A business that regularly sends or receives wires needs a banking partner with reliable wire capabilities and responsive support.

Remote Deposit Capture (RDC): Technology that allows a business to deposit checks by scanning them at their own location and transmitting the image to the bank, without physically delivering checks to a branch. Critical for businesses that receive high volumes of paper checks from customers.

Positive Pay: A fraud prevention service in which the business transmits a file of issued checks to the bank each day. The bank compares incoming checks against the issued file. Any discrepancy triggers a decision request to the business: pay or return? Positive pay is the most effective available protection against check fraud, which remains a leading form of business fraud loss.

Zero Balance Account (ZBA): A subsidiary checking account that automatically sweeps to a zero balance at the end of each day, either funding up from a master account or sweeping excess funds back to it. Useful for businesses that want to centralize cash management while maintaining separate accounts for different business units or purposes (e.g., payroll, accounts payable).

Sweep Account: An account structure that automatically moves funds between accounts based on predetermined thresholds. Commonly used to move operating account balances above a target threshold into a higher-yielding investment account overnight, then sweep them back the next morning. Maximizes yield on idle operating cash without requiring manual transfers.

Lockbox: A payment processing service in which customer remittances are directed to a dedicated P.O. Box managed by the bank. The bank receives, processes, and deposits the payments, typically within the same business day, and transmits remittance data to the business for accounts receivable application. Reduces collection float and eliminates manual check handling. High-value for businesses with large volumes of mailed customer payments.

Merchant Services (Card Acceptance): The infrastructure that enables a business to accept credit and debit card payments from its customers, including point-of-sale terminals, card-not-present (e-commerce) processing, and mobile payment acceptance. Merchant services generate fee income for the bank and are a significant convenience factor for the business. Understanding a business's volume and mix of card transactions helps size the merchant services opportunity.

Treasury Management: The comprehensive suite of services designed to optimize a business's management of its cash, liquidity, payments, and receivables. Treasury management is the full expression of the business banking relationship beyond credit, and for larger businesses, it is often the primary value driver of the banking relationship. The term encompasses most of the products listed above, plus more sophisticated tools like controlled disbursement, foreign exchange, and investment management services.

Payroll Services: Either in-house payroll processing through the banking platform, or through a partner payroll provider. A business owner who processes payroll through their bank simplifies their workflow and deepens their banking relationship. Payroll represents a recurring, high-frequency use of ACH capabilities.

Online / Mobile Banking for Business: The digital platform through which a business accesses its accounts, initiates transactions, manages users and permissions, and monitors activity. For business owners and their bookkeepers or controllers, the quality of the digital platform is increasingly a primary factor in banking relationship satisfaction. Important to understand the business's internal financial workflow when discussing digital capabilities.

Business Credit Card: A charge or credit card issued to a business for operational expenses, supplies, travel, vendor payments. The card generates interchange income for the bank and provides the business with float, reporting, and controls. Business card programs with per-employee card issuance and spending controls are particularly valuable to businesses managing multiple employees with purchasing authority.

Stage 1: The Opening Conversation

Purpose: Establish presence, build initial trust, understand the business at a surface level.

The opening conversation is not a needs assessment. It is a first impression, an opportunity to demonstrate that you are a banker who listens, thinks, and is genuinely interested in the business in front of you.

Keep this stage light. Ask about the business. Let the owner talk. Take mental notes. If a more substantive conversation is warranted, let it develop naturally or schedule a follow-up.

Orientation Questions

"Tell me about your business, how long have you been operating, and what do you do?"

"What does a typical week look like for the business?"

"How did you get started in this industry?"

"Who are your primary customers or clients?"

What You're Listening For

Industry type and operating model. Revenue cycle, does the business bill after work is done, collect upfront, or operate on recurring revenue? Size signals, number of employees, locations, approximate transaction volume. The owner's energy and engagement. Red flags in the narrative: vagueness about the business model, reluctance to answer basic questions about how the business makes money.

Stage 2: The Deposit and Cash Management Conversation

Purpose: Understand how the business moves money and identify early opportunities to add value.

This is where the relationship becomes substantive. Business owners think about banking in terms of their actual problems, cash sitting idle, checks being deposited manually, payroll taking too long, fraud exposure, the hassle of managing multiple accounts. Your job is to understand how the business currently handles its banking operations and where friction exists.

Operating Account Questions

"How many bank accounts does the business currently maintain, and what is each one used for?"

"What does your typical check volume look like, how many checks are you writing or receiving each month?"

"How does the business currently handle deposits, do you come in to the branch, or do you have a way to deposit remotely?"

"Have you had any issues with check fraud or unauthorized transactions?"

Payroll and Vendor Questions

"How do you currently handle payroll, what platform are you using?"

"How are you paying your vendors, check, ACH, wire? How is that process working?"

"Do you have any international payments or foreign exchange needs?"

Cash Flow Management Questions

"Do you experience seasonal swings in your cash balance, times when cash is tight and times when you're sitting on more than you need?"

"What happens to excess operating cash, does it sit in checking, or do you move it somewhere?"

"How are you currently accepting card payments from customers, and how is that working?"

"Do you have multiple people who need access to the business accounts with different permission levels?"

What You're Listening For

Manual processes that technology can improve. Fraud exposure without protection tools (positive pay, dual authorization). Idle cash earning nothing. Payroll friction. Transaction volume that suggests analyzed checking would benefit the business. Seasonal cash swings that will become relevant if a line of credit conversation develops later.

Stage 3: The Business Development Conversation

Purpose: Understand growth trajectory and strategic direction.

The business development conversation is where the relationship shifts from operational to strategic. You are no longer asking about today's banking needs. You are asking where the business is going, and positioning yourself as a partner who can support that journey.

This conversation should feel natural, not scripted. It belongs when the operational relationship is established and the owner has enough trust in you to think out loud about their business.

Growth and Strategy Questions

"Where do you see the business in three to five years?"

"What are the biggest growth opportunities you're seeing right now?"

"Are there constraints on growth, capacity, staffing, space, capital, that you're working against?"

"Have you thought about adding locations, acquiring another business, or expanding your service offering?"

Capital and Financing Questions

"How has the business historically been financed, owner equity, retained earnings, outside financing?"

"Have you worked with a bank on a commercial loan before? How was that experience?"

"Are there capital needs on the horizon, equipment, real estate, working capital, that you're thinking about?"

Relationship and Advisory Questions

"What does the ideal banking relationship look like for a business at your stage?"

"What has worked well and what hasn't in your previous banking relationships?"

What You're Listening For

Timing signals, "we've been thinking about" language that indicates a capital need is forming. Industry and competitive context that will inform later credit analysis. Ownership and succession considerations. The owner's financial sophistication and strategic orientation. Any concerns about the existing banking relationship that represent an opportunity to deepen your own.

Stage 4: The Credit Conversation

Purpose: Explore specific financing needs and determine fit.

Before the credit conversation begins in earnest, one important step belongs here: confirm that your institution is positioned to pursue the type of financing being discussed. The best bankers review institutional appetite before they create borrower expectations, because a credit conversation that generates genuine interest and then produces an unexpected decline damages the relationship. Know what your institution is positioned to do before the conversation goes deep. If a specific loan type or industry falls outside current appetite, have that conversation honestly and early.

Loan Request Questions

"Walk me through what you're trying to accomplish, what would the financing be used for?"

"Is this something you need in the near term, or are you in planning mode?"

"Have you worked through what amount would make sense for what you're trying to do?"

"Have you talked to any other lenders about this?"

Financial Background Questions

"How has the business been performing financially over the past couple of years?"

"Are your tax returns filed and up to date?"

"Do you work with an accountant or a bookkeeper for your financial statements?"

"Are there any existing loans or lines of credit on the business?"

The Rate Question

Business borrowers will ask about rates. Here is the framework to use when the question arrives.

"What kind of rate are we looking at?"

"Business loans are built individually, the rate is based on the design of the loan, our cost to build and carry it, the risk profile of the credit, and the overall relationship. I can't give you an exact number until we understand the full picture. What I can tell you is how it works: we start with a Treasury rate that matches the term of the loan, the index. We then add a margin above that index to reflect our cost and the risk.

Those two pieces together make the rate. Treasury rates move daily, so the index isn't fixed until the loan closes. For a commercial real estate loan, we're generally seeing rates in the range of the corresponding Treasury, five-year Treasury for a five-year loan, ten-year Treasury for a longer term, plus roughly two and a half to three and a half percent. That range will tighten once we've worked through the details together."

The Fee Question

When the fee question arrives, here is how to answer it clearly.

"Are there fees involved in getting a loan like this?"

"Yes, most commercial loans include an origination fee at closing. For a standard loan, the fee is generally around one percent of the loan amount. That covers the cost of underwriting, building, and documenting the structure. On a seven hundred fifty thousand dollar loan, that's roughly seventy-five hundred dollars. The exact amount will be in the commitment letter before you sign anything, so there are no surprises. For more complex structures, construction loans, draws, multiple collateral positions, the fee may be higher to reflect the additional work. And for relationships with a longer history, the full relationship context comes into the conversation."

Rate and Fee Summary

After introducing both components, a natural close to the pricing conversation looks like this:

"The rate and the fee together represent the full cost of the financing. We'll be transparent about both upfront, before you commit to anything. What I want to make sure we focus on today is whether the structure actually works for what you're trying to accomplish. The pricing follows from the structure. Let's make sure the structure is right first."

What You're Listening For

Whether the borrower understands their own cash flow well enough to describe it simply. Whether the request is driven by a genuine business need or by financial pressure. Whether there are existing obligations you'll need to factor into global cash flow. Whether the borrower's expectations about rate and structure are realistic, and if not, whether that expectation gap is manageable or a signal.

Stage 5: The Story Conversation

Purpose: Complete the picture before the formal credit process begins.

The story conversation is not a stage most training programs name. But it is the stage that separates bankers who understand deals from bankers who process them.

Before the application is submitted, before the financial statements are collected, before the credit memo is drafted, you should be able to tell the story of this deal. Not the ratios. Not the advance rates. The story.

> "Help me understand the arc of the business, where it started, how it's grown, and where you see it going from here."
>
> "Walk me through what happens when business is strong, and what happens when it slows down. How does cash flow through the business?"
>
> "Who else is involved in running the business, do you have a management team, or is it primarily you?"
>
> "Are there any aspects of the business I should understand that might not be obvious from the financials?"
>
> "If this loan goes the way you're planning, what does the business look like in three years?"

The Story Self-Check

After this conversation, before any formal application is submitted, apply the Story Test from Chapter 8. Can you tell the story of this deal, in plain language, to someone who has not seen the file? If the answer is yes, proceed. If the answer is not yet, go back and ask the questions you haven't asked.

The Signals That Tell You Where You Are

Business banking conversations rarely announce which stage they are in. But certain signals indicate readiness to move forward.

Stage 1 signal: The owner is engaged and forthcoming about the business. They ask who you work with and what you can do for businesses like theirs.

Stage 2 signal: The owner describes a friction point in their current banking, something that is costing them time, money, or exposure. A specific product or service would address it directly.

Stage 3 signal: The owner uses "we've been thinking about" language regarding growth, capital, or a strategic move. The need is forming.

Stage 4 signal: The owner describes a specific capital need with a defined purpose. The conversation shifts from exploration to evaluation.

Stage 5 signal: The owner is ready to provide financials and move forward with an application. The relationship has been established, the need is clear, and the institution's appetite has been confirmed.

The guide is a map. The territory is the conversation. Every business owner is different, every relationship develops at its own pace, and the banker who follows the conversation rather than the script will build better relationships than one who works through the stages mechanically. Use the framework to make sure nothing important is missed, and then let the conversation lead.

APPENDIX E

The DSCR Quick Reference

Calculating, Interpreting, and Stress Testing Debt Service Coverage

Section 1: What DSCR Measures and Why It Matters

The Debt Service Coverage Ratio is the single most important metric in commercial lending. Not because it is the most complex calculation, but because it answers the most important question: does this business generate enough cash flow to repay this loan?

DSCR is not a guarantee. A DSCR of 1.40x tells you the business historically generated forty percent more cash flow than its debt service required. It does not tell you that future performance will match historical performance. It does not account for risks not yet in the numbers. It is a quantitative test of the story, not a substitute for it.

Used correctly, DSCR is the anchor of the capacity analysis. It should be calculated before the credit memo is written, tested under stress before the credit is approved, and monitored against covenant thresholds throughout the life of the loan.

Section 2: The Building Blocks

Net Operating Income (NOI): Gross revenue minus operating expenses, before debt service and income taxes. NOI is the numerator in the DSCR calculation, the cash the business generates from operations before financing costs.

Total Annual Debt Service: The sum of all required principal and interest payments across all debt obligations in a given year, existing debt plus the proposed new loan. This is the denominator.

DSCR: NOI divided by Total Annual Debt Service. Expressed as a ratio, 1.25x, 1.40x, 0.95x.

DSCR = Net Operating Income ÷ Total Annual Debt Service

Section 3: The Step-by-Step Calculation

Worked Example: Cascade Industrial Supply, LLC

Borrower: Cascade Industrial Supply, LLC. Owner: Marcus Tran, sole owner. Request: $750,000 equipment term loan, 60-month amortization at a rate of 6.75%. Existing debt: one term loan with $38,400 remaining annual debt service.

Step 1, Establish Revenue. Use three-year average where available.

Year	Revenue
Year 1	$2,840,000
Year 2	$3,110,000
Year 3	$3,290,000
3-Year Average	$3,080,000

Step 2, Calculate Operating Expenses (excluding interest, taxes, depreciation, amortization).

Cost of Goods Sold: $1,956,000 (63.5% of average revenue)

Salaries and Wages (non-owner): $412,000

Rent and Occupancy: $96,000

Utilities, Insurance, Other Operating: $74,000

Total Operating Expenses: $2,538,000

Step 3, Calculate NOI.

NOI = $3,080,000 − $2,538,000 = $542,000

Step 4, Calculate Total Annual Debt Service.

Existing term loan annual payment: $38,400

Proposed equipment loan annual payment ($750,000 at 6.75%, 60 months): $88,200

Total Annual Debt Service: $126,600

Step 5, Calculate DSCR.

DSCR = $542,000 ÷ $126,600 = 4.28x

Cascade Industrial Supply generates $4.28 in NOI for every $1.00 of annual debt service, a strong coverage position with significant cushion above the minimum required threshold.

Section 4: The Stress Test

A DSCR calculated at historical performance is a starting point, not a conclusion. Before a credit recommendation is made, the DSCR should be tested under adverse scenarios, because a credit that performs well at base case but collapses under moderate stress is more fragile than the headline number suggests.

Scenario One: 10% Revenue Decline

Stressed Revenue: $3,080,000 × 90% = $2,772,000

Assuming variable costs decline proportionally (COGS), but fixed costs hold:

Stressed COGS: $1,956,000 × 90% = $1,760,400

Fixed costs unchanged: $582,000

Stressed NOI: $2,772,000 − $1,760,400 − $582,000 = $429,600

Stressed DSCR (10% decline): $429,600 ÷ $126,600 = 3.39x

Well above minimum threshold. Credit holds under moderate revenue stress.

Scenario Two: 15% Revenue Decline

Stressed Revenue: $3,080,000 × 85% = $2,618,000

Stressed COGS: $1,956,000 × 85% = $1,662,600

Fixed costs unchanged: $582,000

Stressed NOI: $2,618,000 − $1,662,600 − $582,000 = $373,400

Stressed DSCR (15% decline): $373,400 ÷ $126,600 = 2.95x

Still well above minimum threshold. This credit demonstrates resilience under significant revenue stress.

Scenario Three: Rate Increase (+200 basis points)

Applicable for variable-rate instruments. Proposed loan at 6.75% fixed, rate stress would apply to the existing variable-rate obligations if any are present. For demonstration:

New proposed rate: 8.75%. Revised annual payment on $750,000, 60 months: approximately $94,800.

Revised Total Annual Debt Service: $38,400 + $94,800 = $133,200.

DSCR at +200bps: $542,000 ÷ $133,200 = 4.07x

Coverage remains strong. Rate sensitivity is limited given the fixed-rate structure of the proposed instrument.

Section 5: DSCR Interpretation Guide

DSCR Range	Interpretation	Typical Lender Response
Below 1.00x	Business cannot cover debt service from operations. Cash flow deficit.	Decline or restructure. Primary repayment source is absent.
1.00x – 1.15x	Coverage barely adequate. No margin for any adverse variance.	Typically below minimum policy threshold. Unusual mitigation required.
1.15x – 1.25x	Minimum coverage range. Meets policy floor but leaves limited cushion.	Approvable at many institutions with strong compensating factors.
1.25x – 1.40x	Adequate coverage. Standard commercial credit profile.	Within normal approval parameters. Represents baseline credit quality.
1.40x – 1.75x	Good coverage. Business generates meaningfully more cash than required.	Strong credit. Well within approval parameters at most institutions.
Above 1.75x	Very strong coverage. Business is substantially less leveraged relative to cash flow.	Excellent credit quality. May support more favorable pricing or structure.

Section 6: Common DSCR Mistakes

Using net income instead of NOI. Net income includes interest expense and taxes, which need to be added back to produce the pre-financing cash flow available for debt service. Using net income understates available cash flow, producing a DSCR that is too low.

Forgetting existing debt service. The denominator includes all debt obligations, not just the proposed new loan. A banker who calculates coverage on the new loan only will produce a DSCR that overstates actual coverage.

Using a single year of data. DSCR on a single year is a snapshot. Three-year average or three-year trend analysis provides a much more reliable picture of actual cash flow capacity. Best years cherry-picked by a motivated borrower can produce misleadingly strong DSCRs.

Ignoring owner compensation adjustments. In owner-operated businesses, owner compensation must be normalized. A business owner who pays themselves well below market rate produces artificially inflated NOI. An owner who takes large discretionary distributions through compensation reduces NOI in ways that may not represent a true recurring expense.

Not stress-testing. A DSCR calculated at historical performance and presented without stress scenarios is incomplete analysis. The question is not just what coverage looks like today, it is whether coverage holds when things get harder.

Treating DSCR as the decision. DSCR is one test of the story, not the whole story. A DSCR of 1.40x on a business with severe concentration risk, questionable management competence, or deteriorating market conditions is not the same credit as a 1.40x on a diversified business with strong management and a growing market. The ratio tests the capacity component of the 5 Cs and a G. The full framework requires all six lenses.

The DSCR at a Glance

Element	What It Represents	Where to Find It
Revenue	Total operating revenue, three-year average	Income statement
Operating Expenses	All costs excluding interest, taxes, D&A	Income statement (adjusted)
NOI	Revenue minus operating expenses	Calculated
Existing Debt Service	P+I on all current obligations, annual	Loan statements, tax returns
Proposed Debt Service	P+I on new loan, annual	Amortization schedule
Total Debt Service	Sum of existing + proposed	Calculated
DSCR	NOI ÷ Total Annual Debt Service	Calculated
Stress DSCR	DSCR under adverse revenue or rate scenarios	Calculated
Minimum Threshold	Typically 1.20x – 1.25x	Institution credit policy

DSCR is the quantitative test of the story. When the story is strong and the DSCR confirms it, the credit analysis is doing its job. When the story is strong and the DSCR doesn't support it, or when the DSCR looks acceptable but the story doesn't hold together, the dissonance is always more important than the number. Trust the story first. Let the DSCR test it.

APPENDIX F

The Loan Structure Quick Reference

Matching the Instrument to the Purpose

A Note on This Reference

Commercial loan structures are not off-the-shelf products, they are frameworks built around specific borrowing purposes. This reference presents the primary structures a commercial banker will encounter in business lending. For each, the core purpose, typical terms, key underwriting considerations, and natural bridge to deeper coverage in *Loan by Design*™ are noted.

This is a primer-level reference. It covers the structures you need to understand at the entry point of commercial lending practice. The full depth of each, including specialty structures, combination approaches, and advanced underwriting disciplines, is developed fully in *Loan by Design*™.

1. Revolving Line of Credit

Primary Purpose: Working capital, funding the operating cycle between when the business spends and when it collects. Also used for short-term liquidity management and seasonal cash flow swings.

Typical Term: One year, subject to annual review and renewal. Some institutions offer multi-year commitment periods.

Rate Structure: Variable, typically indexed to prime rate or SOFR plus a margin reflecting credit quality and relationship.

Key Feature, Annual Cleanup: The line must rest at zero for thirty consecutive days each year. The resting period confirms the line is working capital financing, not a disguised term loan.

Collateral: Often secured by accounts receivable and inventory (borrowing base). May also include a blanket lien on business assets and personal guarantee.

Underwriting Focus: Operating cycle analysis, working capital position, borrowing base availability, historical line usage, and whether annual cleanup has been, or can be, achieved.

Watch For: Evergreen behavior (line never returns to zero). Structural use of a working capital line to fund fixed-asset needs. Increasing line balance concurrent with declining profitability.

2. Term Loan

Primary Purpose: One-time capital needs, equipment purchase, vehicle acquisition, business expansion, leasehold improvements, working capital injection at business formation or acquisition.

Typical Term: Tied to the useful life of the asset being financed. Equipment: 3–7 years. Longer-lived assets: up to 10 years. Real estate assets are typically financed under a separate structure.

Rate Structure: Fixed or variable. Fixed provides certainty. Variable transfers interest rate risk to the borrower.

Amortization: Fully amortizing (balance reaches zero at maturity) or partially amortizing (balloon payment due at maturity). Balloon structures reduce periodic payments but create refinancing events.

Collateral: Asset being financed is typically the primary collateral. A blanket lien on other business assets and a personal guarantee are common additions.

Underwriting Focus: Asset purpose and useful life match, DSCR including the new obligation, collateral value and advance rate, guarantor assessment.

Watch For: Term extending beyond useful life of the asset. Balloon maturities creating refinancing risk at a period of anticipated business transition.

3. Owner-Occupied Commercial Real Estate (OOCRE)

Primary Purpose: Purchase or refinance of commercial real estate where the borrower's own business is the primary occupant, typically fifty percent or more of the property.

Typical Term: 5–10 years with a 20–25 year amortization schedule. The rate is fixed for the initial term and subject to adjustment or balloon at maturity.

Rate Structure: Fixed for initial term, indexed to the corresponding Treasury rate (5-year Treasury for a 5-year loan, 10-year Treasury for a 10-year term) plus a margin of approximately 2.5–3.5 percent.

Collateral: Deed of trust on the property. LTV typically limited to 75–80 percent of appraised value.

Key Distinction from Investor CRE: The primary repayment source is the operating business, not lease income from tenants. The borrower's business DSCR drives the credit, not the property's net operating income from third-party rent.

Underwriting Focus: Business operating DSCR including the mortgage payment, property value, LTV, property condition and market analysis, personal guarantee, and any concentrations in the business driving cash flow.

Watch For: Business that accounts for majority of its own occupancy costs, if the business declines, the property loses its tenant simultaneously. Business-specific build-out limiting secondary market appeal.

4. Investor Commercial Real Estate

Primary Purpose: Purchase, refinance, or renovation of commercial property where the primary repayment source is rental income from third-party tenants.

Typical Term: 5–10 years with 20–25 year amortization. Similar rate structure to OOCRE but often with a slightly higher margin reflecting third-party tenant risk.

Collateral: Deed of trust on property. LTV typically 65–75 percent for standard investor CRE.

Key Distinction from OOCRE: Repayment depends on tenant performance, not the borrower's own business cash flow. Vacancy risk, lease rollover risk, and tenant credit quality are central underwriting considerations.

Underwriting Focus: Property NOI, tenant mix and lease terms, vacancy history, market rent analysis, property management capability, personal guarantee, and global DSCR including personal obligations.

5. Construction Loan

Primary Purpose: Finance the construction of a new commercial building or substantial renovation of an existing one.

Typical Term: Matches the construction timeline, typically 12–24 months. Followed by conversion to a permanent loan (take-out financing) at project completion.

Draw Structure: Funds are disbursed in progress draws as construction milestones are completed and verified, typically by a third-party inspector or title company inspection.

Rate Structure: Variable during construction. Converts to fixed at permanent loan closing.

Underwriting Focus: Contractor quality and bonding, project budget and contingency, draw process controls, conversion to permanent loan at completion (and DSCR at stabilized occupancy), guarantor strength, including completion guarantee.

Watch For: Budget overruns, contractor performance risk, conversion uncertainty, pre-leasing or pre-sales assumptions that may not materialize on schedule.

6. SBA Loans (7(a) and 504)

SBA 7(a): Government-guaranteed small business loans for a broad range of business purposes, working capital, equipment, real estate, business acquisition. Government guarantee (up to 75 percent) reduces lender risk and enables more flexible underwriting. Maximum loan amount $5 million. Variable or fixed rate, fee structure includes SBA guarantee fees.

SBA 504: Designed specifically for fixed assets, commercial real estate and major equipment. Structured as a first mortgage from the bank (typically 50 percent) and a second debenture from a Certified Development Company (40 percent), with borrower equity of 10 percent or more. Longer terms, fixed rate on the debenture component. Maximum debenture $5.5 million.

When SBA Makes Sense: Borrowers who do not qualify for conventional financing, insufficient equity, limited operating history, emerging industry, may qualify with an SBA guarantee. SBA also enables lower down payments on real estate than conventional financing allows.

Underwriting Focus: SBA eligibility requirements, business purpose alignment with program guidelines, guarantee application, DSCR typically evaluated on a global basis including all business and personal obligations.

7. Commercial and Industrial Loans (C&I)

Primary Purpose: Broad category encompassing business purpose loans not primarily secured by real estate. Working capital, equipment, business acquisition, partner buyouts, franchise financing, and revolving credit facilities are all C&I lending.

Collateral: Typically secured by business assets, accounts receivable, inventory, equipment, and intellectual property, plus personal guarantee. May be unsecured for strong credits with well-established relationships.

Key Feature: C&I lending is where the custom-built philosophy is most fully expressed. Structure is built around the specific operating cycle, cash flow characteristics, and collateral profile of the individual business. No template applies universally.

Underwriting Focus: Business cash flow, management quality, industry risk, collateral quality (often more dynamic than CRE), and covenant structure that enables effective ongoing monitoring.

Watch For: Collateral that is more difficult to value and control than real estate. Greater reliance on management competence and operational performance as the primary credit driver.

The Structure Selection Diagnostic

Use this as a self-check when a loan request arrives. Start with the purpose. The structure follows from an honest answer to each question.

Diagnostic Question	Direction It Points
Is the need cyclical and self-liquidating?	Revolving Line of Credit
Is the need for a specific one-time asset acquisition?	Term Loan
Is the asset commercial real estate, owner-occupied?	OOCRE Mortgage
Is the asset income-producing property, third-party tenants?	Investor CRE Loan
Does the need involve construction or substantial renovation?	Construction Loan → Permanent
Does the borrower need more flexibility than conventional allows?	SBA 7(a) or 504
Is the need primarily business operating capital, non-real estate?	C&I / Term Loan / Line combination
Is the need complex with multiple components?	See: Loan by Design™

A Note on Combinations

Many commercial borrowers need more than one instrument simultaneously. A manufacturing company may carry a revolving line for working capital, a term loan for equipment, and a mortgage for its building, all with the same institution, often in a combined credit facility.

The discipline of managing a combined facility is straightforward in principle: each instrument should match its purpose, the full debt service of all instruments should be covered by DSCR with adequate cushion, the covenants should be coordinated, and the collateral structure should be rationalized across the full package.

This reference covers each instrument individually. The discipline of combining them is covered in ***Loan by Design***™.

About the Author

Chad W. Maze is a banking executive with more than thirty years of experience inside community banks and credit unions, spanning roles from frontline lending to executive leadership. He currently serves as Executive Vice President and Chief Operating Officer at a large Silicon Valley CA credit union, where his responsibilities include commercial lending operations, enterprise risk, and institutional governance.

His career has taken him through the full arc of institutional banking, from the early discipline of learning credit at the loan level to the later discipline of building and overseeing the organizations that produce it. Along the way, he has hired, developed, and evaluated commercial lenders at every stage of their careers, which is where the content of this book comes from. Not theory. Not curriculum. The patterns he has watched repeat across hundreds of credit conversations, loan reviews, and development conversations with bankers who were good at their jobs but missing a foundation they had never been given.

Banking the Business is the book he wished had existed when he made his own transition from consumer to commercial banking. The ***Discipline of Banking***™ series is his attempt to give the next generation of practitioners what formal training programs rarely do: a framework that actually holds under pressure.

www.ingramcontent.com/pod-product-compliance
Lightning Source LLC
LaVergne TN
LVHW010921110826
845149LV00013B/2439

9798995635932